Follow the Moonlit Path:

Come Home to Yourself
in the
Astrological Fourth House

By Jessica Shepherd

First Edition, 2020
Published by
Moonkissd ☽💋
www.moonkissd.com

Cover:
Image by: Miriam Zilles from Pixabay

This book is dedicated to that deeper call that exists within you. May you listen within, and follow the moonlit path home to your joyous True Self.

Acknowledgements

Foremost, *thank you* to those clients and friends who, over the years, have so widely opened up their hearts, and their fourth house(s), to share their stories with me. You all know who you are! These stories, so integral to the creation of this work, have been used with permission under the condition of anonymity.

Thank you to Catherine Linard, Goddess-sent, for gracefully navigating me through my geographical and spiritual recentering.

I remain eternally grateful for crossing paths with these exceptional people: Steven Forrest, Paul Bogle, Dana Gerhardt - each, in different ways, have inspired and encouraged my voice.

Thank you to editor Gillian Leonard, for her editing talents, and to designer Nada Orlic for executing the cover design.

And finally, to my Soul's mate, Jupiter John, with whom all things impossible become possible and within arms' reach.

Table of Contents

Preface

Astrology in the Aquarian Age

We are living in a period with many distractions available to us. When we stay distracted for prolonged periods, we start to feel disconnected from our innermost selves. This can manifest in symptoms of loneliness, alienation and deep frustration with the world and one's place in it. It's easy enough to see. Look around.

Ironically these feelings of disconnection are occurring at the same time we are able to technologically and mentally connect to more people, places, ideas and events than ever before. Despite all those apparent pathways to connection and information, how connected to our inner selves do we really feel? The art of reflection and poetic contemplation, taking the time to ponder, rest, read, listen inwardly and live soulfully—qualities that define creatively brilliant people and the most advanced civilizations—have been replaced by quicker, faster, more. We have suffered for this in our inner, feeling, life.

In astrology, this current age or epoch encompassing progress, future, science and information technology is called the Age of

Preface

Aquarius. Dissociation from our deeper selves and our humanity are the shadows of this humanitarian sign, which is a paradox since Aquarius is, at its highest expression, an intelligent "for the people" energy that is motivated to improve life for each and every one of us. Astrology is an Aquarian system. In its ability to quickly relay intuitive information, it is an elegant way to perceive ourselves, but any system will be a step removed. Astrology is not a substitution for doing inner work; it is a brilliant tool to enhance it. Yet it is easy to overlay planetary interpretations on our actual experience, which distances our self from the very center we seek. When we hear profound insights about our nature, personality, relationships and path it can be easy to think we are connecting to that Self, without actually connecting to the energy of our present, felt, experience. When we look for certainty, peace or clarity from the planets – or, truly, from anything outside our self - we risk forgetting it always exists, within.

In recent years, due to my own expansion, it has become important to me to ground astrology in my feeling-body experience. To value coming home to myself above all else in my life has also meant that after spending almost two decades as a professional astrologer in some capacity, I made the choice to allow my innate intuitive and empathic sensitivities to take the lead, both in my life and my work.

So why did I decide to write an astrology book *now*? Maybe this is exactly why I chose to write this book now—or it chose to write me! If the birth chart is truly a map of consciousness, the fourth house would be that deeper Source of self from which all of life springs.

In this light, going back to the taproot of the birth chart, the astrological fourth house, makes sense right now. Whereas the Earth's problems and its people are getting louder, requiring our help and innovation, this quiet place of solitude is a worthy metaphor for returning home to our core self. Direct connection with our innermost being happens here, which offers the deep sense of centering, connection and emotional peace we are all seeking.

Taking the time to turn within may look as though we are temporarily turning away from the world, but as with all pursuits of Spirit, this is a paradox. Becoming more centered in the self has practical benefits. When we give our self the privacy to come home, to befriend the part of us who knows the answers to our questions can only arise from taking the time and space to turn within and discover what's there, all kinds of new solutions can, and do, appear.

Your Fourth House: The Great Root System of You

Visualize the birth chart as a great tree. The flowers and leaves are your accomplishments, your worldly works, the goals you have proudly achieved, and your contribution to your community and humanity—essentially, it represents what that the external world may know of you. The "flowers of our life" are found at the top of the birth chart, the Midheaven, MC, or tenth house. The flowers of the tenth house symbolize our worldly works.

Just as a tree cannot flower without nutrient rich soil, sunshine, water and deep roots, you cannot manifest truly great works without being deeply nourished. For the tree, this nourishment arrives through the roots, the great hidden, invisible network that nurtures everything. You have a similarly invisible and self-sustaining energy network. In the astrological chart, your IC, or fourth house, contains your energetic root system - your "come from" in the deepest sense.

To experiment with this idea in your body, for a moment place your attention on your root chakra—the sitz bone connecting you to your seat. Feel the energy there. Your energetic roots extend into the ground below, passing through your chair and the floor, anchoring you into the Earth. How do you feel? Do you feel safe? Nervous, worried? Do you feel connected to those who have gone before you? To the Earth herself? Do you feel taken care of by Divine Source, knowing that no matter what happens, you are okay? Check in with your root chakra energy to know your fourth house.

Maybe you feel basically okay. Perhaps you feel anxious, disconnected, insecure. That's what it feels like to function with a wobbly fourth house. Without this basic feeling of safety, nourishment and rooted-ness, isn't it hard to feel peaceful in yourself, let alone successful, on mission, connected to your calling? To not feel at home within yourself and expect your tree to flower with greatness would be an unreasonable expectation.

But wait a minute, think about how confused we get this. From a young age we are conditioned to focus on mission, marital status, success, and purpose. These are tenth house aims. We are consistently asked the question, "What do you want to be when you grow up?" We are not asked: "How do you feel?" "What do you dream of?" "What do you love to do when no one's looking?" "What do you need in order to feel safe, rooted and loved?" "What home environment nourishes and restores you?" "Who and what is so deeply in your heart that it would take death itself to part you?" (These are all fourth house questions and aims.) Then, when we can't self-actualize or feel stuck in our lives, we end up going to therapy, or on a healing journey—right back into the fourth house!

In the birth chart, and in the energy body, the integral rootedness, centeredness and sense of stability that is essential to the flow and flowering of life energy runs from bottom to top, not top to bottom. If we desire a rich, fulfilling and well-integrated life, why not begin with the fourth house, the root system of the entire chart?

The late great astrologer Dane Rudhyar said the fourth house is one of the most significant and yet least understood houses of astrology. While other, more externally motivated points, like the Ascendant (first house), have been aligned with personhood, whole self-integration begins at the very foundation of our chart. He said, "The astrological character of the fourth house and the planets, which may be located in this section of the chart, should help to discover the best way to reach a state of integration and to acquire a solid, effectual basis for the personality." This area of life Dane Rudhyar described as our center, our very ground of being.

If deepening your relationship to your fourth house offered you a greater sense of integration, centering, stability, peace and clarity, well, wouldn't that be just wonderful? If so, how to begin? We start by turning our attention inward. We reclaim our attention, take it back from the million and one distractions from our self. We start by turning away from the world of Ego, with all its drama, most of it fictional, and toward Soul, a still, quiet place of patient knowing.

Whereas the world loudly drives our focus outward, the fourth house gently tugs inward, to the life of the Soul. It is well suited to the realm of poetry and dreaming, imagining and recollecting, sensitive inner exploration and mythic dives into the deep nooks and crannies of our being. It isn't oriented toward accomplishment or achievement, though both are possible, a happy accident born of inward listening and soulful meandering. The busiest, most exciting and soulfully rigorous days for a fourth house planet may look like "nothing doing" to someone who doesn't have the eyes to see it.

Anyone can claim the treasures of their fourth house. But just as you will find a lover of books in a library, a certain type of person typically heeds the siren call to turn inward: psychologically curious individuals, creative and imaginative types, healers, memory-keepers, those driven to explore personal and collective mythologies and do deep inner work. To us, the fourth house is where it's at. Outer world accolades pale in comparison to the discovery of what's within. Here, a whole world can be found in a flower. I've always loved this quote attributed to Georgia O'Keefe: "It takes time to know a flower, just as it takes time to know a friend." This is a clue to understanding your fourth house. Anyone can get to know it, whether you have planets there or not, but it always takes time to get to know it.

Time, patience, inwardness, soulful meandering…yikes, these are not modern values at all. Our culture may currently be at odds with the inner listening the fourth house requires, but that doesn't mean we have to be. When we don't take the time to pull our attention, interest and energy inward, we risk weakening ourselves, fracturing at the slightest provocation—or news item. Yet a gentle and attentive inward-looking response can help us find center and become the rooted, yielding, unbreakable willow trees that we are.

Preface

In subsequent chapters you'll see me compare your fourth house to an unassuming, loyal, resourceful and imaginative childhood friend. I love this analogy so much. That's how the fourth house feels to me. It contains oodles of talent, magic, whimsy and goodness—a treasure trove of self—but because discovering what's here requires solitude and slowing down, we can easily miss out on what's here. Yet, it's time. When feeling centered is hard to come by, and your very attention has become the most valuable commodity going, when better to befriend the overlooked quiet kid in the room? She or he has so much to contribute to your life and the world.

Just as the talents and whimsy of our quiet kid can remain only in the shadows of our childhood memories, an inner life can go unexplored for decades, or a lifetime. It may niggle at us, though, in the moody language of the Soul, in grumbly dissatisfaction, feelings of displacement, yearning, sadness or a heart tug that something is missing in our life. The fourth house can be easy to ignore, even as persistent feelings of emptiness follow. Perhaps it's time to listen…

Jessica Shepherd
January 2020

Section 1: Hidden Treasure

"I was a hidden treasure longing to be known." - Rumi

I'd always been mystified by my fourth house. What is it all about? What secrets does it hold? Is there a secret handshake or perhaps a special knock required to get in? I wondered, because I certainly didn't understand it. I have a fourth house planet, yet no astrology book description or astrological reading had ever given me a felt sense of it. Cookbook descriptions, in application and interpretation, felt one-dimensional, lacking the magical feeling of self-discovery I've experienced with astrology. And so, historically, I have found the fourth house to be about as mysterious as that enigmatic light that travels our night sky. We look up and wonder...what's up there?

That was the relationship between me and my fourth house.

The fourth house is naturally ruled by or associated with Cancer and the Moon. That mysterious Moon. Sandwiched between the third house (of mind and learning) and the fifth house (of love and creative self-expression), at the bottom of the birth chart sits the fourth house. Astrological houses hold areas of life activity. In modern astrology, it is aligned with our early family and childhood experiences, the people and place we call home today, as well as our inner psyche and innermost self.

Look in any older, traditional astrology book and this is where you'll find your ancestral land and its conditions, family inheritances.

William Lilly says this area shows "profit from the bowels of the Earth." There's farming, patriotism, love of father and land, and the conditions of our retirement. In horary astrology, the fourth house describes the end of a matter, the outcome. Traditional astrologer Deborah Houlding says, "Death by drowning is particularly relevant here." Not exactly encouraging.

I found these a bit hard to relate to, let alone apply to my own experience, and maybe you do, too. Most of us no longer have ancestral homes and lands. Although farming used to be quite common, all the farmers in my family passed on two generations back. Genetic testing has made a comeback and excited new interest, but few of us know our lineage, let alone *feel* the sacred songs, stories and traditions running through our DNA. Death predictions? Those used to be big business for medieval astrologers. It's the twenty-first century and, well, our professions have changed.

Then there's family. For many, the biological family is an alienating or troubling experience. Our blood relatives may not actually be our spiritual tribe, so our spiritual and blood tribes are often two very different entities.

Fewer of us still live in the same places where we came from. Most people move away from the town or city in which they were raised. The mobile state of the modern "home," combined with the dissociation we may feel from our ancestral roots, and alienation from family all make it challenging to know what we are looking at as we view the fourth house.

Thus, began this book—a precarious quest to discover (or rediscover?) the fourth house anew. Within these conflicted and strange bits of information, nothing made sense. Much of what I'd read felt dated, too general for such an intimate area of life, or flat out wrong. How would I ever figure this out? I put this writing away, then pulled it out again many, many times.

Then, one day, I imagined myself bathed in moonlight. After all, the mysterious Moon holds sway over this, a water house. Water is the realm of feeling, emotion, sensitivity, imagination, inwardness. Ah, I was being too mental. This wasn't an intellectual realm. I needed to think less, feel more. I opened my imagination. Instead of looking outside myself for answers, imagining the Moon to be somewhere distant and out of reach, I looked inside, went inward, explored. Eventually, I was surprised by what I found.

Discovering your fourth house is like visiting an old-fashioned, humble tinker who arrives at your village to sell his wares. You are told about a traveler with magic for the strange symptoms, yearnings, needs that plague you. But will you go? If so, you must go in the dark of night to the edge of town, alone. You must learn to feel in the dark, a process which itself feels uncertain. Yet as you investigate and get curious about what you feel, you discover a different kind of intelligent knowing. And soon enough, your tinker guide materializes in a rag-tag gypsy van and you discover there are things you need here, things you didn't realize you need, things that, once found, you wonder how you lived without. Love potions. Handy kitchen utensils. The perfect medicine. That tool you've been looking for on Amazon for months! Maybe, after a conversation with the philosophical and wise tinker, you re-discover a virtue of your own (or another's) character, or a solution to a bothersome problem.

How did you cross this magical threshold, to a place where seemingly no problem exists that doesn't have a ready solution at hand? You stepped into the dark of night, took a leap of faith. You stopped thinking with your mind, trusting your feeling instincts, instead, becoming curious about what you felt and what you might find.

But I'm getting ahead of myself. Begin with moonlight.

My astrological colleague Dana Gerhardt advises her clients to close their eyes and describe who or what is there. "That's your fourth house reality," she says. To enter the fourth house, we need to close our eyes, shut the rest of the world out and enter the realm of intuitive imagination. This is the midnight point of the birth chart, after all. It is dark here. At the time of your birth, somewhere in the world it was midnight, and your sky coordinates—your fourth house cusp sign and planets therein point to that.

Want to get to know me? Wait until midnight, the fourth house suggests. Wait until the world has gone very quiet, dark and still. You'll discover that your thoughts are sharper then, perhaps more poetic. Your energy will be clearer—especially if you live in a big city, since the many Ego energies surrounding you have now gone to bed. What does your Soul yearn for? How are you feeling? What hunger, desire or need calls your name? The middle of the night can be a Soul-revealing time. The world feels softer. Things that seem impossible in daylight become possible. Shadows at the corner of your mind loom larger, mobilize your attention. In that soft, dark night, you will have a direct experience of you—and your fourth house.

A Treasure Hunt

For all its greatness, the fourth house has not enjoyed the sexiest reputation in astrology. While the fifth house, personified, would be your sexy, exciting, popular friend everyone wants to be around, the fourth house would be your faithful, quiet, fallback friend you love to eat midnight ice cream with in your favorite comfy old pajamas when you're tired of going out. There's something comfortable here for you, something familiar, reliable and warm. She or he may not call attention to them self, but they know you in ways that no one else does. For some of us, there's nothing better than this introspective companion who knows our strange, hidden inwardness.

Like your fallback friend, the fourth house suffers from a bit of an astrological PR problem, but this private house is totally unconcerned with PR. Read astrological material about the fourth house, and it's hard to get goose bumps. Family, home, roots, the nature of your retirement years, the quality of your end of life and even death (well, death could be more exciting).

Plus, it's hard to name exactly what goes on here.

I was already many pages into writing this book on the fourth house when it hit me: I've seriously bitten off more than I can chew. Love, Soul mates, self-love, karma…I knew those topics well. But when I looked at my chart and spied Jupiter sitting in my fourth house, I had no idea what to think.

Jupiter, the planet of big luck, blessings and fortune. If Venus is Mother Nature's version of valium, Jupiter is the cosmic equivalent of a cross between Santa Claus and an Olympic coach on steroids. When my clients have a Jupiter transit, I tell them, "Now is the time to believe your own good marketing! Don't think too hard about things, just go for it!"

I love encouraging others to think bigger and to not accept limitations. Developing a worldview (Jupiter/Sagittarius) that includes astrology, magic and spirituality has allowed me to share in this way. While I can plumb my psyche and life for meaning and rich depths, I was put off by the lucky, freewheeling panache and confidence that Jupiter promised, and which I didn't have. Oft colorful, and with a big presence, happy-go-lucky Jupiter typically likes to take up space, be bold, go big or go home. Not me.
I just want to go home. As in, spiritually go home. Or stay at home. Give me options, and I almost always prefer staying home. Always have.

So here was my dilemma. The personality of Jupiter (as defined by most astrology books): extravagant, largesse, expansive, bold, lucky, generous, free-wheeling, optimistic, focused on the big-picture, moral/religious, spiritual. Me: spiritual. Okay, plus one for spiritual.

That this boon of a planet was tucked away in this secretive water house, and retrograde, chaffed me. Studying astrology, one of my teachers, Paul Bogle, told me to look to natal Jupiter or Venus during hard times and hard transits because that's where we can naturally experience some respite and reprieve from the slings and arrows of life. So, of course, during said hard times, I wondered where that comfortable house (Jupiter=big, Home=fourth house) was, and if it would ever exist. At the time, I was living in the Bay Area, in a very, very small and uncomfortable structure, an old construction office, actually, converted into an illegal single dwelling unit. My bedroom was a former closet, my shower a rickety slapdash structure with a sewer pipe jutting through the floor as a drain. On the bright side, it was private and I had a good amount of yard with fertile soil to grow in. I had started an astrology garden, planting flowers representing every planet, from sunflowers whose faces daily followed the path of the Sun, to gladiolas, the upright, sincere funeral flowers for dour and serious Saturn.

Textbooks told me I likely had an upbringing that expanded me in some key way, that my experience of home and family included adventure, higher education, possibility and probably religion. Hmm…a big happy family, perhaps wealthy, well-educated and traveled? No, not that, either. This was not my early experience. If anything, my childhood home felt extremely Saturn-heavy to me: tight, constricted, closed and diametrically opposite the ebullient, expansive, life-enhancing qualities we associate with Jupiter. My fourth house cusp is Capricorn, ruled by Saturn, and mine was in Gemini in the ninth house, which happens to be Jupiter's natural domain. The facts were: my family constantly struggled with money and perceived survival issues and that perception of limitation and lack pervaded the home. Actually, a stifling feeling of *lack* of everything Jupiter stood for—opportunity, abundance, meaning, expansion and unlimited possibility—imprinted strongly onto me and extended well into early adulthood.

When I was born, Jupiter was retrograde. That is, it was moving so slow it appeared to moving backward from the Earth's perspective. Maybe that was the problem? This isn't unusual for an outer planet. Jupiter, Saturn, Uranus, Neptune and Pluto are retrograde a little under fifty percent of the year, and since most of us have a high number of outer planet retrogrades in our charts, I've never thought them all that personally significant. Yet retrograde planets in the natal chart can bring delays to that area, and to the expression of energy.

They are simply slower to act. Is this why, in my life, I could not, would not, see an external expression of Jupiter for so long?

This investigation into the fourth house also brought me face to face with an immutable reality. Viewing any one placement in the chart in isolation from the whole is always a bit dodgy. One principle you cannot get away from in astrology is the vast interconnectedness of everything to everything else; one a-ha moment will inevitably lead to another planet, another connection and another "a-ha!" I was undertaking something that would require me to do just that, to view my fourth house in isolation from everything else in the chart and in myself. This is challenging for most of us to do.

Even so, planets do have distinct personalities. In my experience, these actors of the zodiac are truly like those of Hollywood, magnetic, attention-loving and with a style all their own. They really do want you to get to know them. For instance, give Venus a little sugar—and I know this from experience—she will light up like the fourth of July, opening up to you like a starlet. The fourth house, though? The house a planet occupies shapes how a planet acts, expresses. I was swimming with contradictions again. The fourth house is naturally introverted; Jupiter is not. The fourth house is retiring, private, inward; Jupiter is not. The fourth house is mysterious, an enigma. So, too, was my Jupiter. Finally, on this fact we could all agree.

I needed an approach for this undertaking, a guiding light to keep me on course and from veering too far into uncharted territory without a map. I had two bookcases full of astrology books, several decades of study and professional work, yet I truly felt I had no clue when it came to the fourth house. Frankly, I was tired of the rote definitions that felt dry on my tongue, of fitting together puzzle pieces with inferences that fit sometimes but not at others.

I thought of moonlight again. It occurred to me: I could approach the mysterious fourth house as I would a treasure hunt. I'd use the bones of what I knew, but I'd rely on moonlight to aid my hunt. I liked the metaphor. I'd consult my reliable books, but I didn't want to rely on them. I wanted to allow it to be fresh, let the answers come to me in their way and time.

If I was going to discover the true meaning of the fourth house and what it meant to me, it needed to be a personal journey, similar to one done only in moonlight, in the deepest interiors of one's psychic self.

To do this, I needed privacy, away from the noise and busy energies of the external world. I needed time, to ponder, to gaze deeply into things—as you would if you had a whole day at an arboretum. I needed inwardness, generous permission to look inward and spend time in myself.

To ask the fourth house to speak to me, I would use its methods and poetry.

Clue no. 1: Throw away all the textbook definitions of how you think your fourth house planet should behave. Bathe in moonlight instead.

Of Heroes and Shadows: Your Bio-Family

I have a plaque hanging in the basement of my laundry room. It reads, *Your story begins at home.* I've always liked that sentiment for its veracity. From the moment we are born, it would seem our story is written by nurture, not nature. Our family shows us our first experiences of love, safety, security, as well as their opposites. We are shaped by our family.

Yet those of us who turn to astrology have a slightly wider lens. With a natal chart in front of us, we can literally see that the birth chart existed before our family did. We existed before any of our issues happened. This takes the onus off family—a bit. Sure, we may have actually had a rejecting mother or absent father, but we can also see we were born to expect rejection or absenteeism. The planets are there, telling that story.

I began my treasure hunt at home, with my own early experience. The fourth house is one of the "go-to" methods of getting a bead on our biological family. In astrology, planets/signs in the fourth house describe our early childhood experience, and the most dominant/influential parent. Who was most dominant? The parent who most strongly shaped the early home environment. That was up to me to decide (many astrologers leave the question "mother or father?" up to the person whose chart it is).

I would need to view my Jupiter in isolation from the rest of my chart. Leaving my Cancer-Sun-South-Node-Pluto-Mars t-square hanging there, in suspension, was difficult. It said so much, too. But I could do it.

One of the easiest and perhaps best ways to excavate the true essence of how a planet operates in your chart is by re-reading its mythology. We learn this as beginner astrologers. Myth is the Rosetta Stone of our entire system. In myth, the planets really do become actors, taking on multi-faceted characterizations, subtleties and nuances that set our imaginations afire. I suggest this is where you, too, experientially begin to explore your fourth house, your early childhood and most dominant parent—in myth. You can look on Google or in books. The following is my pieced together assemblage of Jupiter, what I had already learned and what I had forgotten. Retelling a myth you know, in the right time, can be telling on a whole new level.

Astrologically, Jupiter is thought of as beneficent—a "guardian angel" offering protection to an area of our birth chart, and during transits, bestows good fortune in a part of our life. One of Jupiter's nicknames is Jove (Latin for Jupiter), as in jovial, joyous, jolly. Everyone wants to experience a Jupiter transit—until it delivers too much of something we don't want. Too much bad news. Too much food eaten. Too much of a headache. This good-natured, bright, optimistic side of Jupiter is more popularly embraced; his temperamental largesse, the way he blows things out of proportion, his aggravatingly intolerant side, not so much.

See, Jupiter wasn't always the beneficent wish-granter. Jupiter, King of Heaven, had a level of authority and freedom afforded few on Mt. Olympus. As the saying goes, absolute power corrupts absolutely. His stormy, impulsive, grandiose, unpredictable, self-absorbed behaviors befit both King and tyrant. He could be arrogant and greedy, his appetite for personal gain insatiable. When he was in a rotten mood, he didn't hesitate to send thunderbolts flying. According to Ovid, the Roman senate was constantly trying to talk Zeus (Roman Jupiter) down from destroying humanity and the entire Universe, on a whim, because someone annoyed him. Yes, Jupiter was self-righteous, like 1980s evangelist righteous. He was often unrealistic, tyrannical and unreasonable. He was the Boss whose authority and power could not be questioned by others, God, Goddess or human.

I thought about my father. Then I thought about my mother.

Naturally, this good-natured and tolerant slash moodily intolerable and intolerant of others Jupiter had a stormy relationship with his wife, Juno. The tension between his high-minded idealism and her more mundane concerns—like the division of labor in the household, how to parent the children and how to share power in a marriage—constantly plagued them. More bachelor than family man at heart, Jupiter frolicked about with forest nymphs while Juno (Greek name: Hera) grumbled in dissatisfaction about his disdain for laundry and bookkeeping, his infidelities, that he was never home, etc.

As recompense, Juno/Hera was given the honor of most loyal and faithful companion and consort, and temples were dedicated to her, either as the patriarchy's solution to philandering or as a true acknowledgement of the sacred feminine role in maintaining connection. Regardless, women gathered in her sanctuaries for healing during times of marital trouble, and to undoubtedly do what we do with our sister friends when our partners show their difficult, intolerable sides—to bitch, gripe and complain.

10

Not all, but some shades of their royal marriage had played out in my parents' relationship. While my father invested his time and energy into spiritual and university studies, my mother punished him for not living up to her expectations. Like Juno, she used the children, us, as ammunition against him for her many battles. She was angry with him a lot of the time. They fought constantly. My experience of my parents' marriage was more mythic than I'd thought.

Okay, so this fit. But how did this energetic imprint affect me today?

Steven Forrest, in his classic book *The Inner Sky*, says the fourth house is the house of Shadows and Heroes. In your daydreaming moments, what do you fantasize about accomplishing or doing? Rock star? Rock climbing? Rescuing animals? This illuminates the nature of your inner fourth house hero, which you need to integrate into your Ascendant or Mask you wear in the world. When you daydream, who do you become? Do you wear the qualities of your inner hero or heroine in your life, or do you keep them in reserve? This fourth house daydreaming is a form of personal integration.

What of the shadow? The waking nightmares we experience about our self? The shadow is always composed of false fear and shame. It is the story we consistently tell our self, about our self, one that is patently untrue but at one point in time served us in this essential way: we thought we needed it to stay alive. We probably did need it, since so much of childhood requires us to lob off self-parts to insure our parents' love, affection and security. And our shadow points to an area we need help recognizing in our self. Just as it's hard to see one's own backside, the personal shadow is tricky to see.

How did this stormy, all-knowing dictator shape the way I relate to myself?

I thought about my struggle with this Super Ego figure in myself, the one who felt like something was wrong with her when she couldn't meet inflated standards that always fell apart upon scrutiny. So many expectations. So many self-judgments. A constant dark shadow has been an inner sense of "right and wrong." Never toward others, only toward myself, as if my life were being judged by a moral authority on high, and I was always falling short, especially related to intelligence and learning.

Mythically, these observations were psychologically revealing. I could see the large shadow of Jupiter in my Sagittarius Rising father: the intolerant, stormy dictator, the righteous one who knew better than I and did not want to be questioned. I saw how I internalized this figure, in the way I could never "get it right." In the way I expected so much of myself while anticipating criticism at any time.

When I was in my early twenties and first getting to know the rudimentary workings of my family of origin and how they shaped me, this simple information delivered just from the myth alone, about my family of origin, would have fascinated and astounded me with its accuracy. But I'm older now, and because of that, it means something different to me. I'm able to make new inferences. For instance, I have done so much work on releasing old conditioning. I can see how this dark side of Jupiter went deep into my mental patterning and programming. Yet at this age, it really and truly no longer matters who the "judge and jury" that once existed in my psyche was or is. What matters is I am freeing myself from it on a daily basis.

Plus, I do not believe myself to be a prisoner of my childhood.

I remembered a client who was well into her wise crone years when she consulted me. *She was still working on resolving old childhood wounds.* I felt profound disappointment. I wanted her to embody all the wisdom of her years, to be the wise woman who had done the alchemical work of turning base substance into gold, and who was now able to share wisdom freely, a flowering yet rooted tree. I wanted her to be the archetype of wise elder, her experiences having steeped into gentle knowing. I wanted her to be the graceful example, the most positive proof of who we can become, over time, freed into the truth of who we truly are. This was a fantastic projection, of course. I recognized that I wanted this for myself. To finally be free! This wise elder was my own inner heroine. She was/is the person I craved to be, to become. Upon reflection I realized I'd liberated myself from childhood conditioning, family complexes. Having cleansed those ancient wounds, and given them some air, all that's left now is freeing myself from the old habits of thought.

I wondered, if my fourth house planet had evolved from family of origin work…what now? Psychological astrology is a vast subject. The tangled webs of childhood and family conditioning run deep, and some say we are inextricably bound to the work, that the work is never done. The entire chart can easily become a metaphor for childhood wounding and its healing.

While it is infinitely useful to use the chart in this way, my inner heroine knows from experience: we can be free. Our birth chart evolves as we do. As we evolve beyond old habits and conditioning that once defined us, it reveals new facets, new ways of being. I would continue my journey. I would include, in my understanding, the idea that this house holds mysterious familial forces that need to be explored and investigated…but I could see beyond this already. I sensed something deeper. This was the midnight part of the chart, suggesting something mysterious, hidden, perhaps buried. If my Jupiter had been buried underneath the weight of this family story and I was freeing it, who was I *without* that particular story?

Clue no. 2: It's helpful to explore the mythic story of your childhood through your fourth house and planet, but be careful not to get stuck there.

The Dawn of Quiet

"Our culture made a virtue of living only as extroverts. We discouraged the inner journey, the quest for center. So we lost our center and have to find it again." - Anais Nin

I was still struggling with understanding how Jupiter energetically moved and expressed through me, in a concrete and particular way. Mythic Jupiter's personality was magnanimous, extroverted, larger than life. That just wasn't me. In fact, when I was around people with that kind of big energy, it tended to make me want to run for cover, feel different and more alone than ever. How could I connect with the inner experience of my fourth house planet if I didn't feel connected to the planet generally?

Then I was turned on to Susan Cain and her Ted Talk. With the publication of her book *Quiet: The Power of Introverts in a World that Can't Stop Talking*, she voiced things about myself that no one, up until now, had said. Like: Quiet, introverted people are immensely creative and intelligent but they require certain conditions for these traits to flourish—conditions like solitude, privacy, and time to self-reflect, to simply wander in the privacy of one's imagination. Conditions that are not necessarily socially rewarded or supported, and yet introversion fosters character-giving values like patience, integrity, wisdom for culture. And while introversion has not been in vogue for some time now, it has been historically. What permission!

My quiet and privacy loving inner self felt seen. I relished this long-awaited acknowledgement. Collectively, there has been so much noise coming from big talkers with really bad ideas. As Susan pointed out, though, research shows there is absolutely no correlation between being a good talker and good ideas. Intuitively obvious, maybe, but it gave me pause anew. I realized how I'd been conditioned to give extroverts more air time simply because their style was rewarded. This reminded me: the imaginings and crazy ideas of my quiet, introverted side needn't remain hidden. Indeed, they are needed now more than ever, as a balance to the current imbalance.

Thanks to her work, I felt that not only our collective attitude toward introversion, quiet and creative solitude needed to change, but that it could. And thanks to *Quiet*, it finally dawned on me: *Ahh, my Jupiter is an introvert…and so is any planet located in the fourth house!* Reclusive, withdrawn, feeling-oriented, intuitive, soulful, private, secretive, hidden, solitary, inward, quiet, imaginative...these are all fourth house adjectives, too.

I realized I had fallen into the trap of believing a turnip is a turnip. We tend think a planet's energy should consistently behave in a certain way every single time. Mars is Mars is Mars, right? Bold. Courageous. Hot. A warrior. But look at, say, Mars located in the fourth or twelfth house, and major subtleties emerge. Bravery and courage become an inner confrontation with one's personal shadow and demons—*a confrontation which few people, other than the person who has it, will ever know about or see.* A fourth house Mars was not going to be found fighting fires on the battlefields, or in corporate offices, but doing psychological heavy lifting quietly within oneself.

Introverts behave different from the "norm." Water houses also predispose planets to behave differently. The astrological fourth house predisposes any planetary energy here toward deep inner subjectivity. This area is a place of inwardness, quiet and reflection. An area which modern culture doesn't currently prize...but look how well that's going. It's time for a change.

Using *Quiet* and the experiences Cain shared as my new trail guide, I reflected on my experience of being an introvert in an extrovert-favoring culture.

The Quiet Kid

In grade school, I learned something very quickly about life: the extroverted kids were rewarded for their natural style, with praise from teachers for being more vocal, and excelling in group activities, while the introverted kids were not. The extroverts had more friends, and so were popular. Introverts had less, and so were unpopular. Extroverts were chosen first for team sports, and so put in the category of strength and winners. And introverts were always the very last to get picked (we'd rather be reading instead). As a kid, I disliked all sports, and the physical education/gym class for this reason! As an adult, when I discovered I could exercise alone, I learned I actually enjoyed exploring what I could achieve athletically.

Of course, this was all basically okay with me. I didn't want to be the center of attention. Like most introverts, this put me in the path of too much external energy, which would quickly drain me. I preferred the sidelines to the center of the playground. I'd rather be with one or two friends in a sheltering cove I'd created for us, one with a little stream and plenty of room for our imaginations. We could make up games, and don imaginary personalities. We'd bring our dolls. Or just lay down and watch the clouds.

Introverts are not only imaginative, we are sensitive and empathic. In a culture that doesn't value sensitivity, this can be a confusing experience.

I had a best friend who had epilepsy. Once, in music class, she was reaching down to pick up a piece of glitter on the floor when she started seizing. Over and over again, she just kept reaching for that piece of glitter. The class went silent, watching her reach. The air was filled with the self-consciousness you might expect from a group of sixth graders. This moment became burned in my brain. I knew this would make her the subject of childish ridicule, so it was awful for me to witness.

Afterward, her classmates and I learned that if we were ever alone with my friend while she started seizing, we could put a spoon in her mouth to prevent her from choking on her tongue. I clung to this piece of information like a lifeline. But as a result of her condition, many wrote her off as weird. These same groups of kids were also the popular, extroverted ones.

Often ignored and occasionally harassed by the popular kids, I sought comfort in the approval of my teachers and the adults around me. This didn't always work out. I'm not sure if this is the case today, but we used to be graded for things like class participation. There was E for Excellent, and S for Satisfactory and the dreaded NI, Needs Improvement. My teachers often made a point of writing in the comments: *Jessica is too shy, she should speak up more. She should participate with others more.*

Yet I hated raising my hand during class. I could hear my heart pound in my ears. I broke out in a cold sweat. No one, I imagined, had any idea how uncomfortable and unnatural this felt. I can still remember how awkward I felt (and I still feel this way in a group, or on any kind of stage). Occasionally, though, my passion for the right answer or enthusiasm for the subject would momentarily override my discomfort and I'd bravely raise my hand. Later, that's exactly what moved me into a more public realm—creative passion.

This lack of social support continued into my young adulthood. I recall babysitting for a family friend. Years later, my father told me that the husband in the family, a psychiatrist, had once pulled him aside, expressing his concern that I was too withdrawn and shy...too introverted. In this retelling, I felt the old familiar shame creep in about being different. Yet I also recalled the long pauses in conversation when this man would pick me up for babysitting; I felt awkward being alone in a car with an adult male who asked probing questions and who seemed to feel uncomfortable in himself, so I did what comes naturally to introverts: I pulled all my energy inside. As a psychiatrist, perhaps he wanted to stage some kind of introvert conversion therapy? The fact that he decided it was okay to confide in my father about this concern is telling; it is socially acceptable to question the natural style of over a third of the population. It wasn't the first time, or the last, that I was told I should be more...gregarious, openly expressive, vocal or social...different than who I am. I guess he didn't think these things would impair my babysitting skills, as I was still invited to that job.

Interesting thing about shyness. Many people get shy and introvert confused. Susan Cain makes the distinction between being shy and being an introvert. Shyness, she says, is a fear of social judgment. Introversion is more about how you respond to social stimulation.

Extroverts are turned on in social situations, whereas introverts generally need a quieter, low-key and solitary environment for their talents, creativity and gifts to arise. Yet, as I discovered, one can lead to the other. Place yourself in so many stimulating, high energy, extrovert favoring environments with people who expect you to love it and thrive in the same way they think everyone else should, and you will start to fear social judgment and start to judge yourself.

Cain made this point, which really hit this particular nail on the head for me. She said, when you are in an environment that is wrong for you, with its requisite pressures to perform and participate in a certain way versus what feels right for you, *it is actually self-negating for you.* For instance, the current trend toward open office spaces are a nightmare for most introverts, who need to be in their own private space and energy to come to life. Environments that go against my true nature…that felt awfully familiar.

Our society hasn't always been so unfriendly to introverts. That's a recent modern invention. "In America's early days," says Susan Cain, "we lived in what historians called a culture of character, where we still, at that point, valued people for their inner selves and their moral rectitude. And if you look at self-help books of that era, they all had titles with things like *Character, the Grandest Thing in the World.* And they featured role models like Abraham Lincoln, who was praised for being modest and unassuming."

As a child, the adults in my life told me I needed to be a different person: louder, more assertive, more extroverted. Who was I to argue with "everyone"? I certainly wasn't told my way of being was valuable. I wasn't graded for my kindness, my imagination (save for my one creative writing teacher), sensitivity, my ability to entertain myself alone, or my empathy toward others. But these qualities were once regarded as socially valuable, and even aspirational.
For the introvert, the ability to be and work alone for long stretches, to never leave the house, even, gives rise to our particular creativity and brilliance. According to Cain, Steve Wozniak, inventor of the Apple computer, "says he wouldn't have become an expert in the first place had he not been too much of an introvert to leave the

house." I felt that way about becoming an astrologer (the genesis of which began during years of being ill and housebound), as well as my love for the craft of writing, which can only happen in solitude.

I realized I had been asking the quiet kid in the room to be bigger than she wanted to be. I had an inward, feeling-oriented, sensitive fourth house Jupiter, not a flamboyant first house one. I sought adventure and growth in my inner landscape, not in my external persona. There was Jupiter, according to a world of extroverts, and my Jupiter. I was now convinced that these are two very different characters in almost every way conceivable.

The idea that bigger, louder, more is better had been so drilled into me. I hadn't realized how much shame I had carried within for not being that person, whilst not valuing who I am. It simply was not true. This new awareness unraveled that final bit of old cultural conditioning, which told me I should be different (bigger! More talky! Less sensitive! Less introverted!) from who I am…and permission to stop trying to be someone I didn't even want to be.

My Jupiter is in the sign of Aquarius, suggesting I received major social conditioning in this area, and the necessity of its deconstruction and undoing. I had been laboring under so many shoulds—about who I should and should not be—and, as a result, that made me feel separate, alone, different in a negative way. All untrue. In reality, I loved being sensitive, quiet, introverted. I relished deep solitude in a way few people I knew did. All of these traits made me, me. These qualities enabled my imagination, my psychic inward self, to take flight. Yes, this may be different from the norm, but it didn't mean I needed to be anything other than who I was.

I thought I had to be different from who I was. *I was simply different.*

I had deep sea dived for treasure and hit gold. *Quiet* yielded a whole new understanding of my fourth house planet. I had followed its methods. I had done exactly what I thought I, or anyone, needed to do to claim a fourth house treasure: I had gotten quiet. I asked myself some questions. I rooted around. I read books. I asked again, and I waited for answers to arise. I had taken the time to meander through the deep well of my innermost self. I had liberated myself from old conditioning. And no one knew that I was doing this but me.

Clue no. 3: Your fourth house planet is the "quiet kid" who needs privacy and solitude to express its unique gifts, inner treasure and leadership.

The Deepest Self

"I took a deep breath and listened to the old bray of my heart. I am. I am. I am." - Sylvia Plath

Quiet had awakened my appreciation for the quieter experience of myself. My sensitivity, my insightfulness, rightful gifts required a quiet expression.

Having freed myself from misconception, the time was right to look to my fourth house with a more esoteric, spiritual, lens. Besides being a big lug of an extrovert, what else did Jupiter represent? Faith. Spirituality. Perspective. Meaning itself. Jupiter is the part of us who seeks meaning in life, looks at problems from other angles and who, during adversity, is open to considering other possibilities and perspectives that might be useful. Prior to Neptune's discovery, Jupiter was the go-to planet for all things spiritual. Jupiter's greatest gift is an expansive, visionary, quality of consciousness.

I thought about my spiritual resilience, the wellspring of optimism I had internalized over the years. Even as a child, I would think reassuring thoughts like, "I may not understand why this is happening, but someday I will," And, "I know I'm destined for something bigger than I can see now." I had attributed this to the broadening, spiritualizing effect of my ninth house Sun, or maybe just being an "old Soul"; the Saturn-ruled sign of Capricorn, being on its cusp, also holds sway over my fourth house. Yet the idea of Jupiter as spiritual source felt right, too, especially since its located down at the bottom wellspring of the birth chart.

Jupiter inspires us to search for meaning and purpose in our life. Under its auspices we take intellectual, physical and spiritual journeys that broaden our self-understanding, and expand our vision of the universe and our place in it. Astrology has done this for me.

I recalled one of the first astrology readings I received, at age twenty, with an intensely Sagittarius woman (with a lot of Scorpio) who had an appetite for life and later invited me to be her roommate. When she wasn't in a Tahitian sarong, Melissa wore riding pants and boots. Melissa loved horses, tarot cards, stealing pumpkins from church pumpkin patches late at night and telling me that I needed to be more…well, just more everything. She seemed hellbent on communicating to me that she felt I needed to come out of my hermit shell. I wasn't the only target of her aggressive joie de vivre, as she pushed her younger introverted lover to get out in life more, too.

You always remember your firsts. As a seasoned astrologer, if I'd heard this today, I'd not think so much of it, but I was younger then and the first character observations you receive outside of yourself feel soul-piercing. During that initial reading for me, she said, "Ah, you are easily inspired. You don't stay down for long, do you?" I felt that lovely shock of recognition, of being deeply seen. Inspiration was always within arms' reach—in the deck of tarot cards, astrology books, spiritual texts, listening to music, art-making, my favorite depth psychology books. Especially astrology. I had just discovered a system of symbols that filled me with possibility and meaning. There was always something to explore and to expand my vision.

I thought about spirituality and religion, both of which fall under the heading of Jupiter. I'd never been drawn to a formal expression of faith. Religion felt too restrictive, and while I'd dip in and out of Science of Mind services, and experiment with their spiritual principles, I preferred a more solitary spiritual practice: to look within, and to look up. That's how I experience a direct linkage of my

21

path in the pattern of the Cosmos. This does what I imagine any good spiritual practice would. It fosters awe, faith, connection. It opens up a conversation with my deeper self, my Divinity. I can ask questions, here, or I can contemplate the nothingness that is everything. I may not ever attend a formal church again, but I always turn to that temple in the sky. Wherever and however—I always find my Self.

When I added everything up, these abilities—faith in times of darkness, connection to a sense of wonder, the search for elegant universal patterns, trusting in the inherent elegant meaningfulness of things, even when I have no idea what any of it means—shape who I am, deep down. From this vantage point, I could see Jupiter in the friends I call "family"—so many Sagittarians among them—the teachers I study with (always Jupiterian), the subject of books I write, and the life calling that called me. These spiritual gifts may or may not be socially and monetarily valued, but these gifts are what make a life rich, beautiful and meaningful to me. And, as an intuitive guide and spiritual author, they are what I've built my career upon.

What if I'd been drawing from the wellspring of the fourth house all along?

It was like standing too close to the Sun, wondering why you can't see it.

Clue no. 4: Your fourth house is the wellspring of your innermost self—your "come from" in the deepest sense. And so, if you have a hard time seeing it, you're likely standing too close to it.

Then I Met John

Then, in my early thirties, I met John. A jovial academic and world-traveler who ate and drank possibility for breakfast. Someone "blessed with an overwhelming sense of well-being" (his own self-description). I had never, and still haven't, encountered someone more *positively* Jupiterian.

For John, doors open and opportunities grow on trees. I had worked hard on deprogramming childhood tapes of scarcity and limitation from running my life (to which I attributed to, to a large degree, Capricorn on my fourth house cusp), and as proof, here was John, generous beyond anyone I'd ever known. There is always plenty to go around with him. If we had a pie to share, no need to hoard or hide away a piece for oneself…if I, or anyone else in the family, didn't get a piece of the pie, he'd just buy us another one.

It took training to envision possibility for myself, and I devoted a large amount of my twenties to a spiritual path that exercised and developed my possibility and faith muscle. I had thought my spiritual faith muscle was internalized by now, but being with John was an object lesson in realizing that just when you think you're done growing, there's another glass ceiling to bust through. In those early days of marriage, I'd still be too afraid to reach for something exciting, uplifting and growth-oriented. That's too decadent, I'd tell myself about a class or travel opportunity I wanted.

I remember seeing an ad for Steven Forrest's astrological apprenticeship program, and it virtually vibrated off the page. When I casually mentioned it to John, he instantly encouraged and supported me. I just about fell out of my chair. "But it costs money!" I exclaimed. He replied, "I do things all the time for my personal and professional growth. Travel, education, I invest in myself in this way. Why shouldn't you do that, too?" Without that encouragement, I'm fairly certain I wouldn't have tried. John's generosity truly uplifted me in ways I'd never even considered were possible.

Everything changed with my marriage; life took on a decidedly Jupiter tone.

During those early days, I was so high on the energy of expansion, growth and opportunity (and, of course, love). Jupiter and Juno supposedly enjoyed a 360-year honeymoon, and that's how it felt to be married to my Jupiter man. A research academic who traveled the world, Jupiter-John expanded the wings of my ninth house Cancer Sun. Two Jupiterian pursuits, world travel and writing/publishing, became a regular fixture in my life. One thing led to another. As I began to travel, my mind opened, my perception widened, which stimulated my creativity. I found foreign locales and environments, like Viennese coffee shops, nurtured and tickled my muse. Just a few years after marriage, I was producing a blog and writing books.

And there was the house. I have a bevy of Cancer planets, so home is important to me. Till this point, as I told you earlier, I had lived in a house nicknamed *la hermitage* by friends for its tiny size. During our engagement, I surrendered it to John's home, a pink painted house in the gold-covered hills of Marin County, California overlooking the bay. In myth, Jupiter loves wide-open expanses, especially with a bird's eye view, where, all-seeing, he'd sit on a throne overlooking Mt. Olympus. Now, I was on a parcel of land. The house was on stilts, elevated. From our living room window, I could watch birds diving for prey in the canyon, glimpse the San Francisco Bay and see the roads of our small town below. I had the perspective of Jupiter, that wonderful feeling of expansiveness.

Just as my "estate" had increased, so had the size of my family. With my marriage I had inherited three stepdaughters. My family had expanded, now it was almost overabundant. With its notable number of family members and growing (chickens, cats and a dog), our redwood house felt suddenly both big and small, full and tight— which fit with both my expansive Jupiter in Aquarius in the fourth house, and restrictive Capricorn on the cusp.

Did I tell you that John is also zany? Like Aquarian zany. He's a genius, a professor who invents things. He is constantly scheming up ideas, some impossible, and some impossibly brilliant. For every ten ideas my husband has, he says, one actually works, but that's what makes him a delightfully creative and original being to be around.

By all appearances, I realized I had married King Jupiter—but not the patriarchal authority figure. The generous, good-natured version who buoyed others up through his own passionate enthusiasm and lust for living large. I found Jupiter, who had been eluding me my entire life, when I found my true life-mate.

The Secret House of Relationship

"The point of marriage is not to create a quick commonality by tearing down all boundaries; on the contrary, a good marriage is one in which each partner appoints the other to be the guardian of his solitude…"- Rainer Maria Rilke

My marriage opened my eyes to the fourth house in a new way; there was more to the fourth house story than I had previously thought. *Ah-ha! The fourth house is a relationship house*…said no astrology textbook ever.

Except one. Steven and Jodie Forrest, in their book *Skymates*, say "… [our fourth house planet] reflects relationships where we have entered a state of radical, no-exit commitment. We don't really trigger it inside ourselves relationship-wise until we have moved in together under one roof and begun to share our belongings, our money, our routines, our daily lives."

This fit my experience. Before John, I still felt my Jupiter was running at fifty percent and fumes—on a good day. Now life had become…so much *more*. Jupiter's promise of largesse, blessings and abundance finally felt true.

This caused me to reframe everything, and view the fourth house in a new light: as a relationship house, an area of relationship. A relationship house requires the stimulation of another person to fully experience it in all its glory. Similar to the way a fifth, seventh or eighth house only comes really and fully alive once exposed to an intimate other, our fourth house digs a radical commitment, like marriage, or the promise and intention to spend our lives together, to another—one who resembles our fourth house.

Commitment. A word many love to dream about and others dread. Commitment. Because how else do you get to move in together and plan your lives till death do we part? Yes, home, hearth, heart and death do eerily co-mingle in the fourth house. In ancient texts, the fourth house describes the land we live on, who we live on it with (our family) and our end of life. We want to sleep next to this person every night, and if we're extremely lucky, die next to this person, or they next to us. We see the privilege in that.

With a true fourth house relationship, we aren't afraid to commit. We don't have one foot out the door. Foremost, our fourth house partner must share our need to root and settle down. They may share our desire for a "dream home"—on a ranch, island or in the urban jungle—or want to settle down and have a family with no children or pets, to have a home in two places or live on a houseboat. Whatever the fourth house dream, they want to share it with you, and are committed to creating a home together.

This means we aren't in that ambiguous, modern place of moving in together "to see how it works out." We aren't waiting for the other shoe to drop, waiting for that one word or argument or betrayal as confirmation that this person really isn't the One we want to be with for the rest of our lives. This is the home of our chart, the area of life where we feel called to put down roots with another person and to make these kinds of promises: to love one another, and to never, ever leave…at least not willingly.

Of course, life happens, and we may indeed need to part one day. Not all relationships are lasting ones. The best marriages fail, even fourth house ones. The distinction is, right now we want to be with this person forever. Our intention toward this relationship is: "I'm all in." In a fourth house relationship, we put all our chips in, we buy the farm, we take that leap. We *just know* this is the person we want not just right now, but hopefully forever.

I am not convinced one must marry or commit to have a happily nurtured fourth house, but committing to someone or something of a fourth house nature—a Soul family, a brood of furry four-leggeds, a house you caretake with love, a piece of land—infinitely helps. The fourth house comes alive with our nesting urge, rooting, and our undying commitment to love, nurture and care for people, creatures and land, till death do we part.

As a result of my own profound mating, I now believe the fourth house carries the signature of our truest, deepest Soul mates, as well as those people we choose to call our Soul tribe. I'm thinking of a female client who was on a trip with two gay guy friends and was having a ball. "It's nonstop conversation and laughter over here," she said. "Ah," I replied, by way of explanation, "you're hanging out with your people!" She has a natal fourth house Mercury. I told her that those who are youthful in attitude, broadly open-minded, curious, interesting and genuinely interested in you—your thoughts and life—will feel like your people. And that those who were not, were not her people. I could hear my client nodding. Yes, three previous failed marriages were testimony to this, she said. "My ex was only interested in hearing himself talk, not me. He was not open-minded at all."

People who match our fourth house signature are "our people," and because hanging out with people who resonate soulfully and deeply with us moves us closer to our most authentic self, our people will also potentially bring us closer to "our person." Likewise, those who do not match the characteristics of our fourth house signature are neither our people or our person.

Clue no. 5: The boon of your fourth house opens up with your Soul mate or Soul tribe. You can find your people, and maybe even your person, here.

Section 2: Finding Our Way Back Home

"Home is where I want to be but I guess I'm already there..." – Talking Heads

Around the 2016 election (I imagine this isn't a coincidence), I started noticing a theme with clients and in the collective. People felt they didn't belong. Sometimes it had to do with their community, but most of the time it went like this: "What am I doing on this planet? I don't belong here. How could I? This world is terrifying, confusing and sad."

During this time, I remember conducting a session with a woman who basically self-regressed herself back to a prior life experience in a womb-like underwater planet, where she swam with sea life, communicated telepathically and all was bliss. As her guide, I was a bit gob-smacked. I had no experience navigating underwater planets or spontaneous prior life regressions. We had simply asked where the origin of her current problem lay, and there she went, to another dimensional realm where, from all accounts, she appeared to want to go back to that planet and stay there. She didn't want the session to end; she looked so blissed out!

Afterward, she told me she had never felt like she fit in. It was getting worse lately. Not coincidentally, she was also looking for a place to live and was having a lot of trouble finding a place to call home. Currently, she was in a roommate situation she wasn't happy about and, from her self-report, it sounded like a case of history re-

repeating. She had a habit of drifting from town to town, couch to couch. Now, it was reaching situation critical. In tears, she said she just wanted to be back with the dolphins.

"Where should I live?" "Where do I truly belong?" "Who are my family/tribe?" "Why can't I seem to be able to find my right place?" These are pressing fourth house questions. As world turmoil and unpredictability increases, they've become existential ones. In my client work, and in my own life, these types of questions were gathering momentum, speed. I wondered, if the culture of our planet grows increasingly inhospitable, why wouldn't it open up any fourth house fault line we have? Feeling rooted, like we truly belong here, is a fourth house feeling. Feeling safe and protected is also a fourth house feeling. If we have a lingering sense of not belonging here, feeling unsafe, or not being in our right home or with our right people, the earthly pressure we feel today would certainly open up that chasm. The intensity of change occurring on the planet would push it to a head. How could it not, when our collective core stability is being so challenged?

Rootlessness is a fourth house issue, and it seemed to be getting seriously turned up and on by the times. Like my client who wanted to return to her home with the dolphins, we might feel lost at sea, wanting to escape back to a blissful womb-like existence, instead of feeling at home in our self.

Clue no. 6: The instability and changes Mother Earth, our planetary home, is undergoing influence how at home we feel, or don't.

Wandering Navel Syndrome

When our larger Earth "home" feels under duress, we feel it. Whether we attribute this to the people in power and their abuses of authority, the present and looming environmental threats to our planet, or the constant distractions of our technological age, one thing is clear: when humanity strays too far from its *humanity*—our human kindness, compassion, caring and sense of interconnection— we can feel it as disconnection from our self.

I wondered, what happened? How did our priorities get so turned around?

Then I discovered an ancient term to describe what happens when we stray too far from home: *Omphalos syndrome*. I happened upon it in a happy accident, by Googling "navel-gazing." Turns out, "navel," the body part whose sole function is connecting us to a source of nourishment while in utero, is synonymous with omphalos, also meaning the center of the world. From Wikipedia: "Omphalos syndrome describes the belief that a place of material and political power is the most important place in the world." Recognize this syndrome? Our modern world is afflicted with it. It is reflected by our preoccupation with ambition, status, money and power. And yet, interestingly, this syndrome is very old—ancient Greece old.

It is, of, course a symbiotic relationship: What we build the center of our world around and erect structures to, what we decide to worship, give our attention and money to, we also take nourishment from. Even if it has little substantive nutritional value for our Soul.

Constant external focus on Ego preoccupations takes our attention— perhaps the most valuable commodity going today—away from our inner self. Problems occur when we spend too much time outside of our self. Problems like lack of direction and focus, lack of meaningful purpose for our lives, symptoms that may appear psychological in origin, or even appear to be caused by "world problems and events" may actually be a pathology of our external focus. When our worldly preoccupations grow so separate from our inner world of imagination, its spirituality and human values, we become vulnerable. We may suffer symptoms of Soul sickness: lethargy, grief, emptiness, displacement, alienation. Maybe we no longer love, or like, our work. Maybe we feel our home is elsewhere, but not here.

What's the cure for this Soul sickness caused by focus on accomplishment, world catastrophe, power and its abuses, technological devices? Looking inward, listening, dreaming, steeping in the deep self...in other words, navel-gazing. How else to restore power to its rightful place—inside, here? Because, at the end of the day, there are a few things we can change in the external world, while there are so many we can affect inside of our selves.

Navel-gazing. I had Googled this term to understand whether it was truly as derogatory as I'd been conditioned to hearing. An odd term, when I heard it spoken, usually in astrology or psych circles, I always felt a strong sense of shame, somehow dirty or unclean, as if they accusatorily directed the term at me. This was probably because the first time I heard this phrase, it was used against my own inclination toward it. I recalled my mother saying this when she tired of seeing me around the house, which she equivocated with being unproductive. She'd look at me and say, "What are you going to do today, sit around the house and gaze at your navel again?"

What's a navel-gazer, you ask? A navel-gazer is someone who introspects, who, from outward appearances, looks like they are moping, being reclusive, procrastinating, but are actually deeply contemplating oneself, one's life, the conditions of one's birth, an issue, or anything valuable, really. The value of this is invisible to others, and offers no immediate sense of material gain or world accolades or award. Which is probably why this appears in Webster's dictionary: Navel-gazing: "useless or excessive self-contemplation."

Who writes this stuff?! The cards are stacked, aren't they?

And when did excessive self-contemplation become *useless*? Thoreau, Emily Dickinson, Virginia Woolf, Carl Jung and many more great thinkers could be accused of this most heinous act, yet had they not excessively "navel-gazed," what a loss this would have been. In a culture oriented toward outer achievements and power, even our own parents tell us that self-contemplation is clearly not a respectable nor welcomed use of one's time. And yet, someone who chooses to contemplate their own inner life is self-absorbed in the most positive sense: steeping in the deep self. These are the people who hold the light for humanity during times of darkness, who have cultivated the ability to look within and understand the truth of what matters.

I'm a huge fan of navel-gazing. When a client finds their self in the middle of a major life decision, or several, and they have no idea which way to turn, I often tell them to drop everything and take some time off. Do nothing. Stare at the ceiling. Bake cookies. Create a garden. Read books. Make a list of ten things you love doing so much you'd do them for free. To which a client of mine said, "But I can't earn money doing that!" Yes, that is true, but she also had the money to take a few months off. I said to her, "You're not working right now anyway. You could spend the next few months spinning out in survival fears and burn through your savings, or you could generously give yourself permission to explore whatever you want without all the fear and pressure." Permission like that can give rise to a new lease on life, new loves, Soul callings.

It's definitely given that to me. I've spent hours, days, weeks, months navel-gazing. Several times I have made the radical decision to cut down on work hours, and thus my earning power, in order to do spiritual inner work. While it was initially hard to turn away from the convincing siren call of "you'll become irrelevant if you spend too much time inside yourself," the more I permitted myself to obey my Soul's wish, the more balanced and integrated I felt. Navel-gazing has only helped. This takes the form of radical levels of self-care and inner work, hours spent staring into space, writing in my journal, exploring new ideas, writing poetry, drawing, taking walks in nature, being with my pets, having Spirit-based conversations with myself, recalibrating my energies, thoughts. All only ever served me, offering inner stability, purpose, a deeper and more balanced sense of mission.

I stand by my prescriptive advice for the world weary, for journeyers and travelers at a life crossroads, or anyone who is called to soulfully recalibrate—*navel-gazing should be unabashedly pursued in any way it needs.*

Because omphalos syndrome has reached epidemic levels in our culture at large, perhaps more so now than any recent point in history. The preoccupation with shiny things—ambitions, ideas and people who reflect a "get it quick" mentality—may look like it's on the rise, but it is truly on the wane. In a glittery world where what has no substance or character is the norm, rhinestones are everywhere. Yet these disposable shiny idea things fall apart under scrutiny. They do not stand the test of time. Diamonds, though, with wisdom that cuts through mirrors of baloney, have a rare strength. Diamonds are durable under the toughest earth conditions. These diamonds are formed by connecting to the fourth house aims and mission.

Reclaiming our mission by looking inward. Taking time to contemplate what's important. Meditating on virtues of character. Imagining who we'd most like to be. Doing inner work on healing our family of origin wounds. Taking time to read, write in a journal. Holing up in a wooded cabin. All of these give rise to strengths of character, and great ideas, from a soulfully connected place. None of these activities are rewarded monetarily, or given social support. The fourth house has been unpopular; inwardness is not in vogue. Yet inwardness is totally necessary to a healthy species.

Heck, at this point, it's a revolutionary act—in the planetary sense of the word. Let me explain: Halfway through any planet's orbit, that planet is at the point furthest from where it first started, and that's when it begins its return journey, homeward. By this definition, a revolution is not a rebellion; it is a natural journey of returning back home. When we see how very far we've strayed from where we first began, we naturally head back to that origin point.

It can be shocking, though, realizing how far we've strayed. It's like, how the heck did that happen?! If we're honest, most of us can admit that at some point we've experienced this messy truth in our personal life: *Sometimes we have to get very far from home in order to see how far we've strayed.* Without that extreme perspective, we just couldn't see clearly.

It's easy enough to see that, politically, environmentally, we've strayed far from home. When things feel so massively messed up, when it's so easy to feel disempowered, people ask: "What can I do?" The parts create the whole. Or, as some of us like to say in astrology, "As without, so within." What's going on outside is a mirror to the inside.

Look inward. It's worth asking: Do we come home to our self every single day? Or do we distract our self at the cost of our inner, feeling, life? How much of our attention are we feeding the omphalos centers of power and greed? Are we living our life by their arbitrary rules— rules that we didn't create, rules that ask us to go against our self, our truer nature? Do we even realize how far we've strayed?

Clue no. 7: In a culture that rewards external accomplishment, taking the internal time required to come home to oneself is revolutionary.

Family is in the Word Familiar

I deeply understood the woman who wanted to return to a womb-like planet and existence. I had been feeling that way, too. I'd always had the existential sense that this planet is not my home. It was 2016, and the feeling had been growing stronger. I suspect that many spiritual types and seekers often feel this way because we do know that we are temporary visitors here. We remember, on deep, perhaps unconscious, levels that our true home, and our True Self, is one of beauty, ease, grace, light, kindness. When the world appears to be the polar opposite of this, it can get really difficult to live here.

However, this discomfort was reaching epic new levels in the world, and within me. I noticed survival fear and anxiety were the new normal. Deep dread, feelings of panic and fear that were once intermittent in my consulting work had now become commonplace. And, as an energy sensitive, as the people around me were feeling it, I felt too much of it.

Climate change, political messiness, environmental fallout and so much planetary change…this is what we are living with now. Yet people have raised families, created infrastructure and led purposeful lives during very difficult points in history. I knew the world can feel generally tumultuous out there and we can still be okay, inside here.

Finding Our Way Back Home

As one of my favorite authors, Cancerian Elizabeth Gilbert, has said, "This is a world, not a womb." I get it. I'm tough deep down. I don't expect the world to coddle me; I'm a survivor and a pragmatist. I've got Capricorn in my fourth house. Yet as a sensitive lunar type, I'm also super receptive to collective external energies, and I didn't want to be a receptacle for this particular emotional hysteria.

If everyone was in a near constant state of freak out, how would I survive?

Again, I turned to my own inner work to answer this question. What was making me feel so vulnerable to these apocalyptic levels of fear? This constant feeling of being on the verge of panic? Why was it so easy to pick up on the feeling that the world was on fire, and I was no longer safe? For a long while, I slept with one eye open, not fully surrendering to sleep.

Then I asked the question: *When had I felt this way before?*

This was often how I felt growing up. I remember sleeping with one eye open then, too. I had not felt safe. Energies of fear, aggression and panic predominated my childhood, the panic button ever-ready to be pushed at the slightest provocation. These feelings were so familiar to me! The world was on red-alert lately, panic buttons were hair-trigger. Similar to a radio dial tuned into an old familiar station, I easily picked up on that particular quality of energy. I had been raised in these uncomfortable emotional energies, basted in them like a turkey. Of course I would resonate with them again, even though I really didn't want to. *Family is in the word familiar.*

Think about it:

It's in the way we find our self constantly dissatisfied with our home, our living situation—the structure, town or city in which we live—but feel we cannot do better for our self *because we are familiar with lack.*

Or the way we consistently attract a dis-resonant living environment and situation *because we are familiar with not asking for what we need.*

35

It's in the way we feel unsafe in the neighborhood we live in but we won't move *because we are familiar with feeling unprotected and unsafe.*

It's in the way we attract partners and people who resonate with how we were treated as a child, by siblings, parents or even cruel playmates, *because we are familiar with feeling unworthy, unlovable, invisible.*

There's a law of attraction at work. Most of the time we aren't even consciously aware of it. Suddenly, we're thinking negative thoughts, or are overcome by a strange, darkly familiar mood. Like a vampire-energy friend who comes a-knocking when we are at our most vulnerable, and we wonder why we feel so badly afterward, around certain energies we may start to think back to the thoughts of our deepest wounds, thoughts like: "I don't fit in." "I'm alone." "I'm not seen." "I don't deserve better." "I'll never find my true home." Or any variation of our most heinous childhood untruths.

Whatever mysterious energy is bugging you, don't write it off. These yucky stories feel "like home" to us because that is where they originated.

We unconsciously resonate with what's uncomfortably familiar to us. This single concept explained so much to me. In order to feel safe and stable, a fourth house experience, and stop picking up on all that yucky energy, with the help of healer Catherine Linard, I cleared the energy in my family of origin so my energy body finally understood that no matter what I felt, I was safe. I was no longer there.

Having done the work, I still feel the yuck when it's in the environment, but it no longer controls me. I now feel the fear and panic as sensation, and instead of telling a story about it, I can observe it as just energy. Familiar energy, but not mine. Those energies no longer make choices for me. I make my own choices.

Here's the moral of the story: If we haven't examined and let go of old conditioning, it's easy to revert back to those old familiar feelings. My client Marie, in the next chapter, is a dramatic example of how experiences and energies from childhood can undermine our ability to find a home we feel safe in, and a place we truly love to live.

Those Old Familiar Feelings

Have you ever stayed in a situation because your early unconscious conditioning resonated, on some level, with the dysfunction this situation or person so generously offered you? We don't stay in a bad situation for the joy of it. We are *familiar* with it. We do this far more than we realize. With relationships, with jobs, and where we live. We gravitate toward the way our childhood home environment once felt to us. Rejected, neglected or invisible—I'd venture this is a number one reason why, despite being able to clearly envision what we most want in life, we feel powerless to actualize our vision.

Serendipitously, as I began exploring the fourth house in this way, I attracted clients who needed this particular type of medicine. "Marie" (not her real name) was one of my clients from this period.

Marie was being stalked, and had been for several years. She didn't know who was stalking her or why. Since she was a child psychologist who had participated in many trials, testifying against perpetrators being prosecuted for child abuse, she suspected it was related to her profession. It was an awful situation. "They" knew where she lived. She would often come home to find food all over the house, half-eaten sandwiches, liters of soda drunken, clothes strewn about. People would knock on her door, and when she went to answer, there'd be no one there. She was regularly followed as she moved about her day. She had attempted to move to another city (in the same state), but the stalker(s) somehow figured it out and followed her there! This had gone on for so long. She'd hired private detectives and lawyers, and, for odd legal stalker laws I can't claim to understand, the evidence never justified bringing the police or law in.

Marie didn't feel safe at home. When she reached out to me for a consult, her understandable anxiety was severely impairing her life. I was curious about why this had gone on for so long. It sounded extremely uncomfortable, not to mention dangerous, yet she had accommodated this discomfort and lack of safety for such a long time. This suggested something she was familiar with.

Did something similar happen in childhood? Was she familiar with being around danger and feeling helpless and unprotected for long periods of time? Yes. She had been sexually abused by her father, consistently violated in her home—a place that is supposed to be a safe sanctuary and refuge. As a child, she told me, she was denied the ability to draw lines or boundaries on her body, around how she was touched. Now here she was, again, being consistently violated by another unwanted presence in her home and she felt there was nothing she could do about it. The perpetrator would always win.

To me, there was something eerily familiar about this pattern of powerlessness and victimization. I shared this insight with her.

Marie was used to, familiar with, having her will denied. So, I wondered, what did she WANT? *She had this childhood dream of moving to Australia...* Ooh, I excitedly pried, what is it about Australia? Despite never having visited and with no evidence whatsoever, she told me how she just "knew" that she would love it, that she would feel at home and be happy there. She had felt this way since she was a little girl, dreaming where she'd move one day.

We checked the astro-lines (around the globe, we each have planetary zones, or "hot spots," that influence our experience of place) which 100% confirmed her intuition! Australia looked like a really good choice for her. Plus, there were some "big move" transits to her IC coming up: transiting Uranus making a square to her IC, Uranus, and her IC ruler (Sun). This, and the fact she was talking to me, boded very well for a divinely timed move.

Yet, despite her initial excitement at the possibility, she was hesitant to allow herself to explore the steps toward realizing that dream. "It would be too expensive, too scary." "What if I don't like it?" I suggested a visit, checking it out to see if it's viable. And taking a trip to some other potential places, too (she had others in mind). And, I added, "how about really committing to getting the hell out of a home you don't love?!"

She didn't have to voice the many objections—I could feel her resistance. She was uncomfortably comfortable with the old familiar pattern of being violated and feeling unsafe in her own home and body. Yet, wasn't Marie violating herself by denying her own intuition and will to make a big move to another country? If this was true, wasn't she withholding the same protection and volition once denied her as a child from her abuser? I boldly put this forward. After all, in a workplace, relationship, living situation or anywhere, really, holding another against their will is a serious boundary violation (and is illegal). Might we do this to our self, too?

I am not dismissing the fact that she was truly victimized. However, Marie learned from her abuser that what she wanted and needed didn't matter. Now, she was doing this to herself. I suggested that were she to respect her own boundaries by no longer violating the intuitive guidance she was getting from her Soul (and not acting on), maybe then…due to some Divine Orchestration and the magical ways I've seen problems shift or disappear when we finally, really listen to our Soul…this problem would go away.

A light bulb clicked for Marie. She got it. By denying her desire to leave this place that she didn't love, and courageously follow her heart to a home that called to and inspired her, she had made herself energetically vulnerable.

By the way, even though her situation was unique, this isn't unique to Marie. When we don't act on what we know we truly want, crazy walks through the front door. The True Self is a powerfully protective force in that way. When we are aligned with, and make choices from, that place of inner knowing, we are always supported. When we deny acting on, committing to, what we *know* we want and need, we open the door to all kinds of crazy, confusing and sometimes even dangerous energetic influences.

Honestly, no judgment here, because I've done it, too...I've seen the amazing power of both denying one's own intuitive guidance and of listening to and acting on it. Not listening to what you deep down know you want and need is a bad habit because it will invite a level of dis-resonance into your life that only perpetuates drama, chaos and confusion. Even though it feels risky, acting on intuition is a way more fun kind of risk. Acting on our deeper wants yields surprisingly positive results, often beyond our wildest imagining.

This was the opportunity Marie's Soul had been waiting for: to drop victimhood and step into the power of her personal will and authentic self. Now, for the first time, instead of anxiety, I heard true hope and inspiration in Marie's voice. By changing this relationship to herself, she could enter the next stage of healing her early childhood conditioning, which also meant she could choose to move to a home that felt right, safe and true for her. The last time we connected, she had plans to visit Australia and a few other places far away from the unhappy place she'd called home for so long.

Why do we keep attracting a situation or person almost identical to the one that hurt us most? We've been conditioned to resonate with certain difficult situations because they are *familiar* to us. As with Marie, our Soul wants us to re-experience those scenarios so we can restore what was once lost (but never did lose) during the original trauma. Experiences of disempowerment are opportunities to heal, to bring the light of consciousness back to our self.

Nothing is unsolvable, so dire as to not change. When we feel trapped in a situation we feel powerless to change; when we feel powerless and disconnected from guidance, it is so incredibly important to recognize this as just an energy pattern from our wounded childhood. Feelings of desperation, victimization, fear and survival should alert us to the fact that *we are not in present time.* We are vibrating with an old childhood energy—which something or someone in our current environment has triggered.

Clue no. 8: Don't underestimate the power of becoming conscious of your family of origin conditioning. Not doing so can block your ability to find your right people and home…and feel securely at home in yourself.

Uprooted

What had come through for me so clearly, in talking to Marie, was also up in my life. Uprooting was occurring on deep fourth house levels for me, too. I was feeling so vulnerable, so turned upside down by impending changes, and I was feeling a lot of fear around acting on my desires. I was having difficulty obeying the call of my deepest, innermost, authentic self.

After living there for 18 years, I was no longer happy living in California. We'd had a good run, California and I. No longer. Nothing about the place felt good to me anymore. Eventually, almost everything I attempted to do outside of my home, from taking a yoga class to attending a cultural event, sent me careening into a state of physical and psychic distress.

Through energy practices, I was consciously working on clearing old childhood conditioning, and helping my Ego to realize it was safe, that all was permanently well. But as I mentioned with Marie, when we are not making choices from our aligned center, we become vulnerable to strange energies—which paradoxically causes us to feel unsafe. A real catch-22!

I was growing increasingly out of alignment with myself by living here, which also made me vulnerable to picking up the dis-resonant energy of others. If I hadn't known that I am energy sensitive and was picking up on my environment, I would've thought I was the one having panic attacks, because that's how it felt with adrenaline and fear coursing through me.

Other old familiar feelings magnetized me, too: I had never felt I belonged here. I had never felt I fit in. I had often questioned whether I even liked the area in which I lived. Like Marie, I, too, was uncomfortably comfortable with the feelings of dis-resonance I was experiencing. Truthfully, I was too good at tolerating what was intolerable. *Identical to how I had felt in my family.*

Then began the crazy. People started crashing into my car from behind. This happened no less than four times in two years (the Goddess was trying to shove me down the road, onto a new path!) My neighbor, who was mentally ill, started frequently breaking into our house in broad daylight while I was home. Close relationships began to reveal their fractured-ness. People I loved moved away. On one spooky night, while my husband was out of town, a violent rainstorm felled an oak, missing my home office only by a few feet.

I was literally being pushed out. The Goddess Herself was giving me the Divine smackdown. There would be no rest for me…until I left. Later, in retelling my story to others, I learned this isn't all that unusual. Dis-resonant energy is a real force of nature. When it's time to go, it's time to go. No matter how much resistance we have, the Universe operates on Divine Time, not the Ego's timetable.

There was only one thing for me to do: move. But my lovely Jupiter partner told me he didn't want to, that he wanted to wait another five years. Argh! It wasn't a convenient time for it, he said. It was too expensive, and he would lose his retirement benefits, not possible, case closed. I'd heard it all. None of this was true, of course (except, maybe, for the inconvenience factor). In reality, I knew he was deeply unhappy, too, but he wasn't able to see or admit it to himself yet.

Every time we talked about this, he shot me down. We were in a deadlock. I loved him. I needed to leave California. I kept trying to tell him how important this was. He listened, but didn't hear me.

So, after months of communicating all this, one Saturday afternoon while he was eating takeout lunch from his favorite local deli, I took a deep breath and gave him an ultimatum. Even though I'd planned exactly what I would say, I wasn't sure my mouth would obey. I remembered what my energy teacher had told me: Just take a deep breath and speak from your vagina. I planted my feet on the ground. I took a long, slow breath, rooted into my sitz bone, and felt into the pelvic bowl of my female center. I spoke from this deep place of feminine Truth when I said, "We need to move within the year. I'd like for you to come with me. I know your timeline is different, so if that can't happen for you, we need to talk about alternatives."

For me, it was terrifying to issue an ultimatum to my life partner and Soul mate. He was shocked, angry, and a range of other emotions. But I couldn't go on being put off. I was slowly dying inside, losing life force. That is exactly how it felt to me. I had to draw this hard line—for both of us.

There are moments in life when, if you dare to voice your authentic self and stand up for what your Soul needs, even if those you love at first oppose it, miracles happen. Clouds part, angels sing, and Grace visits, with a wink, saying, "Well, why didn't you say so earlier? We've been dying to give this to you..." That's what happened for us. I had taken a deep breath and trusted that voice. I had chosen me, what I wanted and needed, and I had trusted that what was right for me would be right for him. This radically argued with my childhood conditioning in which I was told to put everyone else first.

Back then, John would've far preferred the old, wounded version of me. That person was more convenient for him; she allowed him to hold onto his fear of change. Now, he wouldn't ever want to go back to the old me, but then…then began the inquisition. Him: Asking me to offer guarantees I couldn't give (Where would we go? I didn't know. How could he know that if we moved, settled in, and I suddenly didn't like it, that I wouldn't uproot us again? I didn't know.). Me: Pulling my energy into myself, holding center, reminding myself that what was right for me would be right for him. Plenty of nights I rocked myself to sleep, feeling so alone and uncertain.

I empathized with his incredulousness and mixed emotions; sometimes I couldn't believe what I was attempting to do, either. I joked with my girlfriends, *"Hey, we are moving and we have no idea where we are going. I know, who does that right?! Who decides to tell their life partner 'we're moving, and I don't know where to. Want to come?' Me! I do that now!"*

It was quite a leap. The gamble was: if I trust the call of my most authentic self, wouldn't that guide my life in miraculous ways? I chose yes. All I had to go on was faith and trust that this plan-without-a-plan would work. And very slowly, I saw John starting to wrap his head around it. He had to come to terms with this new plan in his own time and way, but he was trying. He started asking himself what he truly wanted, what his dream vision for himself was. He started taking inventory of what currently wasn't working.

Less than a month later, John traveled to Oahu for work. He happened to mention, in passing, to a colleague, "Jessica would love to live in Hawaii." His colleague said, "Really? The university has some money to spend. You should talk with the director…" And so it went. I mean, the way it slowly unfolded so beautifully and perfectly was nothing short of magical.

Nine months after we had "the talk," he was offered what he calls "my dream job." During this process, he had prepared a vision statement and a spreadsheet with hard numbers, and his new employer gave him no less than everything he had asked for. Talk about the power of asking for what you want—for us both! Sure, there was a lot of uncertainty in the time between, and a lot of hashing it out. We were leaving a place we'd made our home for twenty years, independently and together. We had a house to sell, fears and doubt to work through. It was a bold move coming to an island in the middle of the Pacific. He continued questioning whether I'd be happy, and I repeatedly said I couldn't offer any guarantees.

And yet, within weeks of moving here, we both knew we had come home. Now, he's Hawaii's biggest fan, probably an even bigger fan than I am. He's come full circle, and can't imagine not being here. He now tells anyone who asks, "I love it here so much. I'm never going to leave."

Driving into our new neighborhood on that first day we were greeted by a full rainbow, either end so close you could practically reach out and touch the mythical pot of gold. Overwhelmed by the warm Aloha greeting, and the feeling that I was finally home, I broke down into tears. It was the first of many times I would cry tears of happiness and relief in those first months. I was finally home. My new mailing address: "Dorothy, end of the rainbow."

Did I happen to mention that I moved to my Jupiter (expansion, growth, prosperity) line? The same planet that, for so many years, had totally eluded me? It seemed to me that karma had just served me my just desserts—a thank you for my faith, patience and belief in myself.

Rumbles in Your Hidden Center

The fourth house. According to evolutionary astrology, it exists only in our psyche. Few people will ever truly see or know it in us, only those with whom we are willing to share our pillow and toothbrush will know it. It is invisible, hard to put our finger on, and unless we have the time and inclination to go meandering, the bright, shiny things in the world will distract us and we could miss it altogether. And it is so quiet here. (Can you hear the pin drop?)

Yet there is a time when the fourth house makes itself clearly known: during an outer planet transit. Do you want to know how you *really feel*—about your loved ones, home, family, your life? Have an outer planet fourth house transit. Saturn can certainly do this, too, but when the outer transiting planets connect with the very foundation of our birth chart, rumbles are definitely heard and felt far and wide, and in all corners. Suddenly, those fault lines that we'd been glossing over with strawberry icing? The Gods smile, or smirk, as if to say, "Well, what did you expect? That's not superglue, my dear."

Maybe we don't have fault lines, maybe we just have little fissures or hairline fractures. We feel those. Any cracks in our foundations are definitely felt. It feels big. It's all coming out, or up.

Why are fourth house transits so pivotal? Because the fourth house is connected to the four cardinal angles of the birth chart. I have always found the angles of the birth chart fascinating for this reason: they are inclined to act. The angles are movers and shakers of the birth chart. When planets connect with them, events happen. If you're an impatient person by nature, don't worry about having to wait around very long. Stuff will go down: home, new decisions, relationships, career… Visually, look at the chart and you can see that this bottom part of the chart is foundational to just about everything.

This is the foundation of the entire chart. Since transits to the fourth house angle can affect every single area of your life, it can make your knees shake. Just as a great tree shakes in a violent wind and rainstorm, if there is rot, nutrient poor soil, or other diseases within the system, sometimes the storm uproots the entire tree itself. If you've seen an uprooted, felled tree, you can just feel the vulnerability of it. During times of stormy change, your fourth house can hold you up strong, or leave you feeling exposed and vulnerable.

The beauty of a fourth house transit(s) is that we do get an opportunity to realign to a deeper, more authentic Self source. This is wonderful, akin to a rebirth into a truer version of yourself. The difficulty, at least initially, is it's stressful. Family, high emotions, issues with home and marriage are all common at this time. This is an invitation toward deeper individuation. To shore up fault lines, areas we haven't been totally in alignment with our self. To course correct where we've gone astray. To implement a more solid structure, we need to figure out where things have become weakened.

Astrologically, what was happening for me when I uprooted our lives and moved to the middle of the Pacific? Transiting Pluto (death/transformation) had just made a square my Moon (home) followed by transiting Uranus (dramatic awakening) square my IC. Meanwhile, transiting Saturn was opposing my IC ruler, also Saturn.

Lastly, Jupiter just made a square to my IC from the first house. Lastly, transiting Pluto was about to conjoin my IC. The very day we stepped foot in our new home was also the day that Pluto in Capricorn made its first exact conjunction to my fourth house cusp.

If you just glazed over while reading this, don't worry. I list it all here to make a point. The more transits to the IC—or fourth house cusp, or their ruling planet—the bigger the changes. I was having so many of them! During this time, huge core shifts are occurring. Whether you move home or not, these massive planetary energies will find a way to move you.

So, while, yes, you can get to know your fourth house on any old lazy Sunday afternoon, outer planetary transits to the IC and/or fourth house arrive with a sense of urgency and inner pressure that make its presence unmistakable and imminent. There's no mistaking the fact that we are being called to integrate at a whole new level. As our inner foundations are tested for viability, our life for its true Source-centeredness, we make major discoveries, often startling ones, like: *Hey, the foundation I have built my life and reality upon? Well, that is no longer true for me. It's not working!* Then, the question becomes, *What now?* Or maybe even, *Where to?*

Clue no. 9: A fourth house transit will expose the fault lines in your foundations. This necessary uprooting will align you with your truer self.

Where Should I Move?

This is a question I encounter in client practice, and, of course, which I myself had for quite a while. The whole idea of choosing where to move stupefied me. I knew what I liked in a place, and what I didn't...otherwise, I had no idea.

Since everything is energy, including planets, why not dip into astrology's ability to illuminate the kind of energy we might encounter not only in our current living environment, but in a potentially new one?

Astro-mapping comprises a handful of techniques that allow you to follow the globe, so to speak, to different experiences of your same self. The most well-known technique, astro-cartography, was developed by Jim Lewis. Let's say you were born at sunset in Italy, which means your natal Sun is located on the seventh house cusp, or descendant. At that same moment, in Japan, the Sun would be rising (ASC). In San Francisco, it would be high noon in the sky (MC), and in Bombay, it would be midnight (IC). The rising, setting, noon and midnight points correlate to the four angles of the birth chart: the rising or Ascendant (ASC), the setting or Descendant (DSC), noon or Midheaven (MC) and midnight or Imum Coeli (IC). Astrologers plot these rising, setting, noon and midnight points onto a special map with zones, or areas, where planetary energy can be quite strong. Simply put, your Moon, Sun, Mercury, Venus, Mars, Jupiter, Saturn, Uranus, Neptune and Pluto lines alight at different places all around the globe. Your experience of a place, including your home, will be influenced by your proximity to these lines.

For instance, if you're living on your Neptune line, as I was in California, you may find your explorations of spiritual consciousness and creativity come into high focus, and are well-supported here, while health, sensitivity, escapism and illusion are potentials, too, if you have those vulnerabilities—since Neptune rules all things glamorous, invisible and hard to put your finger on.

As tempting as it is to be so literal, one person's lemon can be another's lemonade. It all depends on how you relate to that planet in your natal chart. For instance, my natal Neptune is quincunx my Cancer Sun, which suggests health issues and low vitality. Neptune has been a tricky energy for me to navigate, not always a friendly one. Yet another person will have a different experience. Your experience of your planetary line totally depends on how you relate to the planet, which you can explore in great detail using your natal chart (not just

48

the astro-line itself). A client with natal Neptune in her first house lived on her Neptune line and had the most amazing, positively spiritual experiences working with dreams and healers. She had a friendly relationship with Neptune, indicated by a trine to her Sun. A Leo Sun friend with Neptune in Scorpio in her relocated first house said she always feels "invisible" in her town—despite having an otherwise extroverted chart! She has Neptune in her natal twelfth house, square Sun, and figuring out Neptune is a bit murky for her.

Pluto is one planet that gets a lot of bad press, but, here again, one person's bitter tonic is another's cup of healing tea. One client booked a session because she wanted to move but she had no idea where she wanted to live. I asked, where was your most favorite home located? Of all the places she had lived in her life, she waxed on about Virginia Beach—her Pluto line! Pluto isn't for the feint-hearted; it can be a demanding energy requiring rigorous self-honesty, letting go of outworn Ego attachments and a few trials by fire. When I told her this news, she was horrified and exclaimed, "Not Pluto! But I hate drama and transformation. I just want calm." Apparently, her Soul had other ideas. Her natal Pluto in Leo was located in her fourth house. As she reflected, she said she had many transformative experiences in her former Plutonian home. By her own admission, it appeared her Soul really liked a level of intensity and transformation.

Despite what one might think, not everyone is drawn to move toward their Venus (ease, harmony, love) or Jupiter (expansion, blessings) line. Neither are we necessarily drawn toward the planet or ruler of our fourth house. Why? Our Soul has an evolutionary intention that is always best served by a particular quality of energy, and at a particular time. In the above example, I didn't assume my client wanted to live on her Pluto line, though I could see it was located in her natal fourth house, indicating a level of Soul alignment. So why wouldn't she want to move to a Pluto line? Wouldn't she feel more at home there than anywhere? She might be in a phase of life requiring her to interact with another energy for a while. If we are having a planetary transit, a transitory energy is asking us to integrate that energy into our life for a period of time, so we may be drawn to a place with that particular energy. We might call that certain planetary line home for a while, then another place home later.

Indeed, she was having a Uranus transit at the time of our session, and was intuitively drawn to places on her Uranus line. It often happens this way. The places we are intuitively drawn toward reflect the energies we are ready to integrate on a deeper level.

In another example, I had a client who was experiencing a Neptune-Moon transit. Guess where she wanted to relocate? To her Neptune line. Neptune wasn't in her natal fourth house. Her story? She had achieved great professional and financial success as a co-founder of a major recognizable household brand. She had made loads of money, and career-wise was at the very top of her game, but she had become disillusioned by material things, success, and was ready for a new phase of spiritual exploration. She and her young husband decided they wanted to follow their guru to open an ashram/retreat center. How great for spiritual Neptune! I felt perfectly at ease advising her to go for it. Her current life goals were totally in sync with what the planetary lines suggested. Did it last forever? No, she did not stay in that place. She eventually moved on. Yet it worked for her for a time.

Should you move to your fourth house planet? Or should you move to the line of your current big planetary transit? Confused yet?

As I hope you've discovered by now, while we can learn the quality of energy of our current and potential home, and we can use our transits and our fourth house to see how this all matches up, the astrology can't tell you what to do. Astrology can't possibly know what your Soul wants for you right now. Only you know that. Choosing where to live is an intuitive process. Knowing your planetary lines can help you tune into your intuition.

I happened to be experiencing a Pluto transit to my IC, the point of home, when I moved to Hawaii. I was moving during an extremely Plutonian time of my life. Yet I moved to my Jupiter, not Pluto, line. I didn't move here *because* my Jupiter line was here, though I did know it. I moved here because things easily came together, doors opened, and it felt right to me—all signs of being at the right place at the right time. I also paid attention to the quality of energy I experienced while here. To me, Hawaii has always felt expansive, generous, giving, blessed. It continues to feel this way.

I never advise basing a big move solely on an astro-mapping reading; I suggest visiting. Firsthand experience is truly the only way to know whether a place feels right. Plus, few people know how to interpret the information, and even astrologers can misread things. Descriptors on internet sites like astro.com are general; since they do not take your individual relationship to the planets into account, it can be confusing. You really do have to rely on your own self-knowing!

Are you ready to look for a new home? If so, I will leave you with a final thought, based on my experience with this: If you have been living in a dis-resonant energy, vibrating in that "old familiar feeling," when you visit new energy, it may be hard to know up from down and left from right. We get used to those old feelings of angst, or not belonging, and as uncomfortable as they are, they are also familiar.

When visiting Oahu on my recognizance research trip, I knew I really loved it here, but I also didn't feel things "click" yet. I actually said to myself, *No, this doesn't feel quite in alignment.* Luckily, I gave it time to unfold. I knew it felt so different from what I was familiar with, and since the old familiar hadn't been working for me, I suspected something different could be really good. Think about it: If you want to change a habit of being drawn to unhealthy relationships, the next person you date or befriend will probably feel strange because they don't fit the former mold, right? And wouldn't that be a good thing?

Clue no. 10: When looking for a new home, exploring your planetary lines is worthwhile and fun, but keep your intuitive knowing in the driver's seat.

Go Where Everybody Knows Your Name

"Sometimes you want to go where everybody knows your name, and they're always glad you came…" - Cheers theme song, Gary Portnoy, Judy Hart-Angelo

On a trip to Miami, I made a new friend, Suzy, from Jamaica, her native home. My husband had recently visited the island, and over cocktails one evening he described the frustrating and comedic experience of running all over the island trying to find a new contact—someone he was told he just had to meet. Yet no one could agree on the person's name. Richard, who drives a Ford Pinto, who has crazy hair and lives on the other side? Oh, you must mean *Tom*…

Chuckling over his experience, Suzy explained how difficult it is for a visitor to figure out where exactly a person lives in Jamaica. It's not an information issue; there are phonebooks, the Internet and mail. The problem is Jamaicans have two names: a given and real name. The given name was given to a child by their parents. But, she quickly explained, people call you by your real name, which often has no resemblance to the given name. You'd think it would be an abbreviation like Rick for Richard, but that's not the case. Instead, Larry Smith might have a given name of Chester Johnson. So, if you do not know where Larry lives, lots of luck. You'll have to drive around the island and describe "Larry" (he's five foot seven, is married, has five kids and drives a Buick) to everyone, until the guy on lunch break from the banana factory where he also works says, "Oh yeah, that's Chester—he lives on Montenegro Avenue."

What potential for confusion, this dual name system! Yet it also struck me as so incredibly fourth house because it maintains a distinct line between relationships in our lives. Only those people who know us intimately will ever know our given name, and the rest will have to spend the day driving from banana factory to banana factory.

Likewise, only those who know you intimately will ever know your innermost sanctum, your private fourth house Self. They will know that you shop when you are depressed, how you take your tea, your dream of living on a tropical island, your secret crush and that you have territorial issues with your controlling mother. They will know that, even though you show up to the world in a very different way, you are really a closet mystic with an enduring love for all things spiritual who reads tea leaves and tarot in her spare time. In other words, our fourth house people will know our *real name. They know the real "you."*

That's the beautiful thing about the fourth house, we feel deeply seen by one or a small handful of other people. These are the people we call our Soul's mates—our Soul or our heart's family. These are the people who know our real name. How different this is from the Facebook-y world of social media, where so many people can know of us but so few actually do.

As the ancient house of old age and death, the fourth house whispers to us that our time here is limited…so we may as well spend it with one who truly sees us. Not just our social personality, our role in society or in relation to others, but people who see, love and know the entirety of who we are, to the degree that we can ever fully be known by another. People who truly know us would have something substantial to say about us at our funeral. Yes, that kind of knowing. These are the people who belong in our fourth house tribe.

At day's end, we only want to be where someone knows our real name.

Section 3: Follow the Moonlit Path

"Remember the sky you were born under, know each of the star's stories. Remember the moon, know who she is." - Joy Harjo

I had reached a point in my treasure hunt where I felt fairly satisfied in my understanding of my own fourth house. I had followed that tickling intuitive nudge in my belly to explore a few ideas about what the fourth house might, experientially, mean. I had taken the time to meander down those moonlit paths, which, besides the bits I knew from years of study, were illuminated only by inference, imagination, shadows and light. I allowed my eyes time to adjust to the moonlight, my senses to open to insights, clues and keys. Adding these to my map, I had followed these trails to see where they'd lead.

I felt my journey had come to a good place. I'd arrived at a place of intimacy and knowing. I better understood how to nourish my innermost quiet, private self. Like every good journey should, this one left me feeling full, spent, and it had left me a few unexpected surprise treats. It had given me permission to be okay with being different from the norm. It had given me a sense of *belonging*, to myself, which I write about at this book's end.

As I learned about the fourth house, I learned how much I truly loved spending time here. I love staying home, being private, solitary, only letting a few chosen few Soul mates in. These have become personal truths, not just liabilities of living in an often harsh, too loud world. I love my sensitive and feeling nature, which allows me to deeply see into others' hearts and Souls. I gained a newfound respect for wanting to protect my Soul's sanctuary.

Not to mention, I no longer felt cheated out of my Jupiter experience. I discovered the treasure buried here, a spiritually contemplative Jupiter, full of valuable life experiences and wisdom. I wouldn't underestimate it, or the fourth house, again.

I could see how my fourth house (Jupiter) nature was also mirrored and supported in my choice of life partner, and the Soul tribe I am naturally drawn toward. I could see the ground I'd covered: how I'd worked through some major family of origin conditioning, and recognized the more evolved, positive expression of Jupiter in my chosen family today. I could see how planets transiting my fourth house were Divinely orchestrated for my benefit, helping to remind me that it was time to deeply integrate again, to uproot, recenter and create a more supportive foundation for myself.

Now came the time to illuminate your fourth house planets and signs, to share some of these gleanings about your fourth house with you. The undertaking seemed awesome and enormous all over again. After all, look at how extremely personal and subjective the fourth house is! Look at the amazing, not to mention lengthy, journey this one planet had taken me on!

I reviewed what I had learned. The fourth house spoke in whispers and whimsy. I had used the means and methods of the fourth house to explore it: imagination, intuition…and some astrological knowledge about the archetypal experience of the fourth house. Beyond that, I was in the dark. I had followed a moonlit path, laid a breadcrumb trail for myself. I gave it all time to percolate, because the fourth house, perhaps more than any other, requires our time…time away from external demands. If I followed these fourth house methods, I trusted that something would appear.

I don't claim to know what exactly resides in your fourth house. It's too personal of a place. I cannot write your story for you; you write your own story. But in getting closer to it, I hope to give you permission to explore it more fully. The planetary symbols are like Moons of their own. That is, each shine a specific quality of energetic light to your fourth house experience. As they shine their golden-silvery cast in the ways they do, and your eyes adjust to the moonlight of your planet(s), out of the corner of your eye you may see moths suddenly liberated out of shadows and into the light of awareness, or caterpillars morph into butterflies. You may discover what you thought was a barren field was actually a dormant one waiting for the right nurturance and sustenance from you. Under that glow, you may discover a long-lost sense of playfulness, light and whimsy.

The Moon is interesting in that way. All kinds of things can appear to be different from what you had thought. In tarot, Moon is the archetype of illusion. In the moonlight, what looks like a dragon can actually be a dragon fly. A triple-headed hydra can be a finger puppet. What you think you see depends on the play of light, shadow and your vantage point, which may not resemble reality at all. And so it goes within our mysterious psyches. Our fears and scary stories are often just distortions of the moonlight.

I now present to you my most humble undertaking: I imagine what story your fourth house might tell about you. My moonlit meanderings about your planets are a starting point, inspiration for you to take your own journey. I deeply love, value and appreciate the soulful fourth house in ways that I hope you will feel jump off the page—and into your Soul—too. So, as you read on, take your time. Rest. Stop at the scenic points. Reflect. Sit by the moonlit well, allow your own insights to emerge. There's no better method for finding the treasure hidden deep, right inside here.

P.S. If you need help identifying your fourth house, please turn to the Appendix at the end of this book for a mini-instructional.

Explore Your Fourth House: Planets and Signs

Before we head into the passages describing planetary archetypes, here are the general guidelines I used for this exploration. However, just as no one but you can ever exactly and precisely know what resonates with your true experience, it is a rough sketch, not a full picture. Allow the below ideas to guide your own intuitive process.

Your introverted Quiet Kid resides in your fourth house. He or she needs you to create a certain environment for you, for them, to thrive.

In grade school, we all had quiet friends, or maybe we were that friend. Remember him or her? The quiet, smart, imaginative, funny kid who made you laugh till you peed, who you'd tell all of your secrets to, who you could always count on as a lunch companion? Who was often last to be chosen for sports, but first choice when you were feeling lonely or needed a true friend?

You may recall that this friend, the one who "just gets me," was also the one whose talents, voice, skills and abilities were often obscured by louder, more extroverted others. They weren't popular, not by arbitrary social standards of lunchroom school politics. They weren't invited to the cool table. They probably did not run for school office or join the cheerleading squad. They may've been called weird by "other" kids. Yet you *knew*. This was one of, if not the, funniest, warmest, most interesting people you will ever meet.

The quiet friend of your Soul who "just gets me"? The hidden and sometimes strange talents they had, that you believed in even when the world couldn't see it? You did not leave this friend behind in grade school. She or he is *you*. Here, and waiting for you to find—in your fourth house.

Fourth house planets are that quiet kid. Naturally introverted, they prefer quiet places, interior spaces, the world of imagination. They need a certain environment to flourish and flower, and they rely on you to create that. Your fourth house planet and sign will tell you what you specifically require, but general rules apply: your quiet kid needs solitude, privacy, and plenty of freedom to explore what they like, in a manner that feels most natural. This freedom will always give rise to expression of talents, skills, leadership, gifts that may've gone unnoticed had you forced conformity to a social standard.

The fourth house is where you can restore and renew yourself.

The fourth house call is mysteriously evocative. It's like finding a long-lost world you always knew existed but needed a bit of moon magic to enter. You might need faith, as with Neptune/Pisces in the fourth, to enter. In this case, maybe the inner passageway will open for you by reciting Rumi poetry, or lazy days spent in bed reading your favorite authors, or journaling your innermost thoughts, or tracking the cycle of the Moon herself.

Your siren call will be unique. The sign/planet combination describe what form of magic to call on. Many, especially those with fourth house planets, will be called, only to discover that the more time we spend there, the more time we want to spend there. It's a hungry house. It would be. We live in a solar world that values achievement and material success. Imagination and reflection, those fourth house processes that give rise to great and soulful creativity, are celebrated only when they're commercially lucrative.

As you consider what restores and renews you in a deeper way, give yourself permission to be whimsical, light, and not goal-oriented. In other words, if you discover there is a secret mystic in you (Neptune/Pisces in the fourth house) and she or he craves your attention, do not say, "I want to explore my spiritual and mystical side, but maybe before I invest in that intuitive development course, I should see if I can make a living at it."

Instead of staying in the "how?" focus on the "what?" What am I deeply curious about? What calls me? Allow your heart intention to replace external goals and see what happens.

The fourth house hungers for imagination and soul-making. A poem, play, or great novel are merely byproducts of that rich inner exploration, a record of the journey into parts of self as yet unknown. Through the processes of reflection and introspection, key features of the fourth house, we are rounded out, made into fuller, more integrated human beings. Often, following this moonlight gives rise to a *Soul calling*—the best kind.

Your fourth house describes your Soul's mate(s) and Soul tribe.

The fourth house tells us as much about what we need living under one roof as it does about the type of person we can stand to live with. They may even be interchangeable: our partner is always changing up their food and routines at home, and lo and behold we have Uranus in our fourth house, which is anything but business as usual. This is by design. When our partners resemble our fourth house planet, a special compatibility ensues. They like the way we decorate the house, or we agree on parenting styles. When it doesn't, we tend to experience rumbles of discomfort in our bellies. We don't feel at home living together and may find it altogether intolerable.

In astrological synastry, the astrology of compatibility, you might find your truest Soul mates resemble your fourth house in key ways. For instance, if you have Venus in your fourth house, they may be Libra or Taurus, or have Venus strongly placed or emphasized in their birth chart, and so on.

If the phrase "Soul mate" doesn't work for you, not to worry; we find our *Soul's mates* in the fourth house. When we further widen our definition of Soul mates to "Soul tribe," we open ourselves up to even more possibilities. The archetypes in our fourth house tell us how we can create our spiritual tribe.

All of our fourth house companions are our *soul's mate*; we may call them family, we may call them our Soul tribe, or life partner, but they are definitely friends of our Soul. They have a special ear for our inner whispers. They know things about us that no one else does. They speak the secret language of our heart. Over time, they

59

understand things about our personal history, and how that shaped us. They are our tribe, they know all the names by which we are called, and they may have a special name just for us.

Your fourth house describes your personal "om"—what you need to feel centered at home and with close companions.

What is your ideal home? Is it a spiritual sanctuary full of natural light, spiritual objects and meditative alcoves (Neptune)? Is it a salon full of lively conversation, friends, family and neighbors coming and going (Mercury)? Or perhaps it is a place where you and your partner do as the poet Rilke famously said two lovers should do, "protect one another's privacy"? Does it have boundaries, and plenty of space for solitary explorations (Saturn, Pluto)? The sign and planet(s) here describe the well-protected safe haven environment we seek to establish with our new family.

Do we need a partner who will respect our privacy and solitude, one who is comfortable during those long stretches of silence we will need when we're called to do inner work? Do we enjoy a lively, stimulating home environment with plenty of discussion, socializing and lots of communication? Busy or serene, no matter the nature of our fourth house planet, one thing imperative for any planet located here is: privacy. Even if you live in a revolving door commune, you will want to be able to shut the door for privacy's sake from time to time. This protected space is inherent to the symbolism; our own "sacred home space," located at the midnight point of the birth chart, is the farthest you can get from public view.

Home is a sanctuary, and when it contains all the right elements to nourish your Soul, it will also nourish the Soul of your union.

Your fourth house points to unhealed family patterns which, if not addressed, can create: rootlessness, difficulty settling down with a life partner, or prevent you from forming new bonds altogether.

Our family lineages are long. The water houses hold the energies of our ancestors—their unrealized dreams, untapped potential, wounds, unfulfilled longings—and may want our acknowledgement.

Family skeletons don't always show up in obvious ways. They sort of slip in, and often into the current day marriage. Have you ever felt the presence of a partner's mother or father in your marriage? Have you known someone who's said, "I feel like my spouse's mother's ghost is here"? My father told me numerous times that my maternal grandfather's ghost was a strong presence in their marriage. Remember, ghosts aren't always spectral apparitions; they are psychic and energetic phenomenon that can be felt in present time. Family of origin healing work is a huge preventative here.

In respect to the astrological houses, I've found that people with a planetary emphasis on the natal fourth (and eighth) houses, especially, carry a special legacy for the family. It's as if for the fourth house person, the ancestors are part of a larger Soul group whose evolutionary goals are similar in key ways. A fourth house Soul may have a need or desire to grow through an experience that their ancestors have also similarly faced. Often, the ancestors are helping from the other side (and more than happy to help if you ask!), offering the fourth house person both the gifts and burdens of what's been unrealized. Once you start digging, the parallels can be eerie!

I explore this concept more deeply in section four of this book.

Your fourth house has buried treasure. Protect and cherish this treasure, but don't forget to share it with the world.

Remember the quiet kid who always sat at the back of the room? They were so quiet, even though we secretly knew they were the funniest person in the class. Maybe they were just shy (afraid of social judgment), or overwhelmed by other kids' energies. Perhaps they didn't like the way joining in with groups also meant they couldn't do what they liked. Or maybe they really came alive in more intimate environments. That's our fourth house planet.

There are a hundred and one reasons why we might not want to open up and share what's inside, at least not until the right time, space and place, but a risk every introvert, and every fourth house planet, may…eventually…want to take is to sharing all the goodness that's inside. Once we dial in that right environment, the right activity and people, it gets easier to do.

"I was a buried treasure longing to be known…" This quote is from the mystic Rumi. I myself felt this way for a long time. I felt I had so much inside that I might burst, that I didn't know how to express. Then I found writing. I found astrology. I found people who spoke, and loved, the language of the Soul. Jupiter, my fourth house planet, is correlated with Sagittarius. My third house (writing, language, learning) has Sagittarius on the cusp. This area proved an avenue for me to open up, expand, learn, grow, let others in. I finally felt myself known, my gifts seen and shared. While inherently inward with a predilection for solitude, I now know my fourth house planet has as much to offer to the world as any other, if not more. As you explore your fourth house, I wish the same discovery for you.

Pro-tip: In addition to identifying the house your fourth house planet rules, looking to the area your fourth house ruler is located allows you to play with where (and how) you can unpack your buried treasure chest—and share your fourth house gifts with the world.

Questions

Q: What if I don't have a planet in my fourth house?
A: Look to the sign on the cusp, and ruling planet, of your fourth house.

I remember when I first moved in with my fourth house Jupiter mate who openly professed to want to give me the world on a platter. Yet when I needed to replace the "house of futons" (literally) with something more comfortable, he was all up in arms. His excitement about me joining the household was palpable, but if I moved a picture or chair a little, he noticed it right away and behaved as if I was an usurper of his power and kingdom. I was mystified at his mixed signals. His Venus is in the companionable sign of Libra; did I really have to teach him the art of compromise?

Eventually, I learned that after divorcing his first wife, he wanted to make this new house a real home for his daughters, so everything he had acquired, no matter how utilitarian, had the energy of this "single dad" identity and rite of passage. Getting territorial and defensive about me acquiring a new sofa was a form of self-protection and a demonstration of this fierce protectiveness toward his lion cubs. He was warrior-protector of this lion's pride…and he was still healing.

My partner has zero planets in the fourth house. But territorial Aries rules his fourth house cusp. His Mars, Aries' planetary ruler, is in Cancer, the sign of home, heart and family, reinforcing this sharp nurturing energy. Mars falls in his sixth house of daily routines. He can be particular, and dislikes change. In our household, he likes things to stay where he put them! He has hero-warrior energy about him, loves being called into action or battle on behalf of loved ones, embodying the protector-provider of this combination.

In other words, he very much embodies the Soulful Warrior I describe in the section on Mars/Aries in the fourth house!

In a nutshell, planets are energy, and a planet in the fourth house will express more energy here, than not. Simply, if you have a fourth house planet, you have an evolutionary contract to fulfill in this area of life. However, while not everyone has a fourth house planet, everyone has a fourth house sign, and a fourth house ruling planet (these are one in the same; Aries is ruled by Mars, Taurus and Libra is ruled by Venus, and so on). So, read for your fourth house sign. Then, consider the sign and placement of your ruling planet, if you know it. Ruminate on, explore what you learn from, these descriptions. See what you identify with, and what you can pull together on your own. All create a fuller fourth house picture.

Q: I'm an introvert, but I have no fourth house planets? / I consider myself an extrovert, but I have fourth house planets?
A: You don't need to have fourth house planets to identify as an introvert.

63

And if you are an extrovert with fourth house planets, you may stand to value your introverted nature a bit more than you do.

Not all introverts have fourth house planets, and not all people with fourth house planets identify as introverts. Introversion describes your orientation, by degree; we all fall at different places on the introvert-extrovert spectrum. Yet a fourth house planet will always be introverted by nature. This means if you feel you are more of an extrovert, but you have fourth house planet(s), you might give extra attention and care to your planet. Since you favor extroversion, which is typically more culturally and socially supported, your introverted side is likely more easily ignored or neglected.

Likewise, if you consider yourself an introvert but you have no fourth house planets, your fourth house sign and its ruler offer important clues about how to more deeply affirm, nurture and support your natural tendencies.

Q: These are natal descriptions, but I'm having a fourth house transit. Can I also read this as I would a transit to the fourth house?
A: Yes, but run it through the filter of your own fourth house first.

Because a well-tended fourth house is the bedrock of our entire life, when it needs attention, everything can come to a grinding halt so we can address what's being asked of us. No one understands this better than someone who is experiencing an outer planet transit to their fourth house. Suddenly, it feels like the bottom drops out from under us. A parent gets sick, or our marriage, home life or our very identity starts receiving mini-earthquakes. Trying to move through the world "business as usual" with a moving and shaking fourth house is like trying to walk on ice wearing tennis shoes. It's doable, but extremely difficult. When your core stability requires a radical re-evaluation and re-alignment, you can feel unstable from the inside out.

Yet you have a basic ground, a basic core stability that you can reliably sink into. No matter what is happening in the moving sky, this will always be *your* natal fourth house. The transiting planet is more like a cloud passing through, carrying an energy you will need to integrate and become familiar with for a time, but its endpoint is in service of *your own* fourth house.

Foremost, read for your natal fourth house sign and/or planet. This will always be most relevant, since the planet transiting will stimulate your entire fourth house and its placements. If, for instance, you have the Sun in the fourth house, and Pluto is currently transiting your fourth house, you cannot separate your experience of transformative Pluto from the fact that this profound time is inextricably bound to your self-expression (Sun). Though the stimulus is outwardly Plutonian right now, solar type acts will be required of you. Read for the Sun. Then read for the transiting planet, knowing its character will be the same, but since it does not have the same permanence of a natal placement some features may not feel relevant. For instance, you may identify with the idea of no longer avoiding hard truths right now, versus it being a lifelong contract of your Soul.

By now, I hope you can see that a fourth house transit is a perfect time to get to know your astrological fourth house, all over again—so good on you if you're experiencing a fourth house transit and reading this book!

In summary, your fourth house describes:
-the home atmosphere that nurtures you, the energetic nature of your home
-your quiet, private, introverted side the external world doesn't know or see
-the archetype(s) of your innermost—private, quiet, introverted—self
-specific energies and actions that recharge and restore you to center
-your Soul's mates, those you want to commit to, settle down with
-dreams, whispers, fears, longings only voiced to those who know you well

In its moonlit shadows, you may discover:
-old familiar childhood conditioning patterns preventing you from feeling centered, rooted, finding your Soul's mates and your heart's true home

-a family curse, secret or legacy, and a need for you to do ancestral healing
-inner resources arising from mysterious spiritual and psychic inheritances

Transits to the fourth house: mobilize your attention on core needs and values, ask you to look inward, can feel like the rest of your life is in suspension. Disruption, uprooting, inner reorientation. Home and family (as emissaries of Soul) dominates attention. Matters feel "close to home." Look to your natal fourth house planet and sign as guides for this period.

Sun in the Fourth House, or Leo on the Cusp:
The Bright Recluse

Lara had always been a bookworm as a child. While the other kids were out being social, she hid in her room, her imagination nourished by flights of fancy. As she grew up, her introspective and thoughtful nature blossomed and she gravitated toward inward-oriented companions like herself, people whose inward nature gave her the privacy and respite she enjoyed. When she met her future husband, she was attracted to his quiet reserve, his gentle silence that complemented her own. She felt so comfortable around him; they could sit side by side for hours in companionable silence. Whereas others could interpret this as dull or lacking in stimulation, they were happy simply growing old together over time and sharing one another's dreams. Their bond ran deep and true.

If you were born with the Sun in the midnight part of the birth chart, in prior lives you may have led a public life where everything you did was subject to public scrutiny, or that of an authority figure, and the development of a personal life unfettered by obligation and commentary just wasn't an option. Likely, what you said and did, where you went and who with, was put under a microscope. In a nutshell, you lacked privacy, and time to yourself.

As a karmic balance, in this lifetime you're turning inward, digging deep down into what's most important and valuable to you and only you. You often prefer the sound of silence and exploring your own thoughts, imagination and ideas to the color and fanfare of the outer world around you. This doesn't mean you can't appreciate or desire the solar world of ambition and professional recognition, but you are psychologically oriented to pay more attention to your inner world than the outer, which is by design.

To do this, you need privacy and autonomy; privacy to maintain your separateness and draw boundaries if needed, and autonomy to explore your interests, what captures your imagination and what fills you with a sense of purpose and gladness. Just as we all are happier and in brighter spirits on a day filled with sunshine, ideally, your inner search—your interests, inward-looking journeys and creative explorations—light you up, vitalize you. They bring you a sense of clarity about who you are and where you are from.

Restore and Renew

To restore and renew yourself, draw from the infinite well of creative being. Often, fourth house Sun people are prolific readers of books. Books are amazing for their capacity to take us on an inner journey of self-discovery without ever leaving home. If you are curiosity-driven, you might enjoy taking up some form of lifelong study, as it allows you to embrace your solitary nature for long periods of time, which energizes you. Whether spending time in nature, with books, studying something that fascinates you or creating, take long and regular drinks from the cup of yourself.

You need private time to steep in your true self, but you aren't necessarily a hermit. Having a fourth house Sun will not make you resemble, in habit, say, Henry David Thoreau, the author, naturist and essayist who "went into the woods because I wished to live deliberately" (we don't know if Thoreau had a fourth house Sun; he was a Cancer Sun sign). Though this idea may sound absolutely fantastic to you! You may, over the course of your life, come to prefer solitude more and more because it agrees with you.

You can still experience renown and fame if that's your path. By no means does a fourth house Sun exclude you from fame or recognition, if that is your wish. After all, the fourth house is the natural house of the Moon, which is the Sun's creative counterpart and complement. This combination is a signature of creativity, and can engender great magnetism and public sympathy. The public is drawn to those whose deeply personal values and ideals want to make themselves known to a wider audience. Humanity is eternally hungry for compassionate, imaginative, inward-looking Souls who lead through the example of their own inner life experience, and the values they form as a result of having lived from a deeper, truer place. For instance, Michael J. Fox, a fourth house (Gemini) Sun, after being diagnosed with Parkinson's disease, is now its spokesperson. Some astrologers say fourth house people will achieve a deeper sense of creative satisfaction and fulfillment after mid-life. Perhaps that is because it takes time to become who we are. Plenty of musicians, writers and artists, people who give voice to the life of the Soul, have fourth house planets. Likewise, anyone who feels a strong sense of "personal calling" in their life is drawing from their fourth house taproot.

Your Soul Mate(s) and Tribe

Generally sunny, optimistic, happy go lucky—these are a few of the ways we describe a well-nourished Sun. These descriptors can also be applied to your partner, because your fourth house planet will reflect the qualities that help you to feel at home in yourself, and in your actual home environment, and the people in it.

The Sun, by nature, is its own entity—its own sovereign. It doesn't ask for permission to be itself, to shine, it just does it. On the highest end, your solar fourth house mate is one hundred percent their self, their own person doing their own thing, lives life through their personal values and offers the same to you. A marriage and home environment where two people are fully free to be their selves is a beautiful thing. One person moves the lamp or sofa, and the other doesn't get tied up in knots. An opinion is expressed, and the other doesn't take it personally. Since the fourth house Sun is so deeply connected to their values, shared values always help this partnership.

Most importantly, shared values bring a quality of spiritedness and independence to the partnership. Ideally, your mate is self-contained and has enough of a life to not get underfoot at home, and in your space. There's a need for privacy, for you both. Your partner need not be a solar person—in fact, they may be rather private. They may enjoy hanging around the home or just contentedly doing their own thing in the garage, office or garden. Equally, they can be a more public figure, too, and that is because the Sun does like to shine. The most public person can be deeply introverted and a homebody. Introversion is a defining quality of energy you both share, not a job title.

The Sun here suggests your dominant parent took up a lot of space and light when you were a child. You may've felt eclipsed by their attention-seeking nature, or the way they lived their life seemingly unconcerned about others. On the bright side, their strong sense of self may've given you security; you always knew where they stood. Whether you agreed with them or not, they were straightforward about their values, ideas, and you could count on that.

If you have difficulty taking up space and shining in your own right, or you tend to feel dominated by others, it may mirror your relationship with this dominant parent. It's a good idea to take a hard look at certain issues, before settling down with a partner. Like, how you may unconsciously expect to be overlooked, or your habit of making yourself smaller. Otherwise, you may find yourself with a partner who mirrors this conditioned feeling of being overshadowed.

On the least effective spectrum of expression, a Sun person's partner can be Ego-inflated, believing their self to be the center of the world. An egotist is no fun to live with! In this case, the individuality, desires and wants of all family members are perceived as threatening to the person holding the reins. This is not the right approach for a fourth house Sun person, whose individuality, autonomy and self-expression must be valued and celebrated by all fourth house mates. In fact, they will always find their biggest cheerleader at home.

There's No Place Like Om

Sunny, warm, inviting, just like the Sun, your home is a place full of good cheer. Ideally, it has your personal signature in it. Have you ever

70

visited a home that looks like it's a page taken from a catalog? That's not for you. You need to look around you and see precious mementos and cherished treasures, all of which reflect your unique personal color and style. After all, you charge up your batteries, your life force, here, so your home environment needs to subtly or more overtly reflect your own energy, taste and style. If you are looking around you and seeing the style of your fourth house mate written all over the walls and floor, you know what you need to do!

Your home should include your partner's tastes, too—certainly don't take over the space. If you are too attached to leaving your mark, it can be a point of contention with your home-mates, in which case you may need to step back and look at your desire to override others. However, your Soul tribe may give you full-on permission to do so because it's what you desire. In the domestic sphere, your self-expression wants to be given full and free rein. Whether that means working creatively from home, or surrounding yourself with art of your taste, domestic projects make you happy—and reflect you.

This planetary placement draws from the wellspring of deep self and family. Writer Jane Austen famously chronicled her life in a close-knit family; she had a fourth house (Sagittarius) Sun. Family is important to you. Even if it's not family in the traditional or biological sense, you appreciate the grounding, history, continuity and window on yourself that being deeply bonded to a small tribe gives you.

Since your very identity revolves around roots, hearth and home, you appreciate a partner who has a similar inclination. They might be close to their biological tribe, or place a high value on the family you've created. Your chosen family may have a handful of two-leggeds or four-leggeds. Pets and animals are members of your Soul tribe, too! Privacy-loving by nature, you can take your time finding someone to let in. But chances are you'll find at least one two-legged to settle down with over the course of your life. The person who wants to put down roots and create a home and family with you, who isn't scared away by the promise of "forever," is the right person to bring into your fourth house love den.

Your quiet kid could be a/an: artist, natural performer and entertainer, shy lover, creative go-getter, clown or jokester, innocent at heart.

Your fourth house mates: are introspective, rooted, prioritize home and family life, honor your creative autonomy, respect your need for privacy.

Your fourth house mates are not: rolling stones, commitment-phobic, domineering, egocentric, disrespectful of your need for privacy.

Ancestral healing: release ancestral blockages around creative expression, creative autonomy and willpower. Someone in your lineage may have taken up the spotlight in the family, eclipsing others' expression. Heal this by reclaiming your natural joie de vivre and confidence. Follow your creative enthusiasms. Share your natural light, and your inclination toward joy.

Your hidden treasure: your creativity, passion and enthusiasm for what you love, the natural-ness and ease you experience in yourself when you are doing what you love—yes, doing what you love—what lights you up, is all you'll ever need to place your trust in. It is your sturdiest rudder, your guiding star and light. Think about how easy it was as a child to simply be yourself, to shine. No second-guessing. No "self-esteem issues" (what's confidence and self-esteem to a child?!). Go for it. She/he's still in there!

Moon in the Fourth House, or Cancer on the Cusp:
The Hidden Healer

Phil's happiest memories involved his family's ranch, where the cows would graze under a sky as blue and wide as the ocean and the laughter of his childhood trickled like the mountain brook. As a child, visiting the ranch with his cousins at summer, catching tadpoles by day and fireflies at night, was a favorite formative experience. Now, as a psychologically self-aware adult, he realized that he often tries to recreate the easygoing dynamic he had with his family. In his close friendships, he always sought out people who shared his irreverent sense of humor and who easily expressed the emotional warmth, kinship and loyalty that he had experienced during his early days. Some might call his closest companions "friends," but to Phil they were more than that—they were his Soul tribe.

If you were born with the Moon in the home and family sector of the chart, in prior lives, or in this one, you lacked the stability and rootedness of a place to call home. Perhaps you lived as a rolling stone, moving from one place to another. Maybe you were forced you to leave your homeland, or had to leave your clan behind. Whatever the case, now it's essential that you re-establish that severed connection, as it's a basis for your very emotional security.

Pay attention to your yearnings. Maybe you have Soul memories, emotional yearnings or nostalgia for a place you call home, or a desire to spend time whiling away the hours in your imagination, enjoying domestic pleasures of food and family. An idealized childhood home or dream house might come to mind, or, as with Phil, there was a place in your childhood where you felt totally safe, free and loved. These urges, memories and images serve as anchors, drawing you inward toward soulfully tending your roots. Establishing a safe place allows you to let down your guard and heal.

Restore and Renew

The Moon is the great healer, and you have a gift for healing. People feel comfortable bringing their problems to you. You have a therapeutic effect on others, and you don't even have to open your mouth—it's your very presence. Your sensitivity to others, the fact that you care, is apparent in your energy body.

While this is a real gift, it's often the case that the person the healer first needs to heal is their self. The fourth house invitation is to heal any neglect your feeling-nature suffered as a result of trauma, or not having spent enough time at home, looking within, and tending to your own wounded child (lest not to attract lost, wounded Souls). You have an emotional need to recharge and renew yourself on an ongoing basis, to give yourself the room and space to be alone with your feelings. As you restore a sense of stability to your life, with time for inwardness and self-reflection, you develop palpable emotional authority and self-awareness, and attract this in others.

This is a very subjective, feeling-oriented placement for the Moon, which lends itself to creativity, private hours spent whiling away at pleasurable creative and imaginative pursuits. Paradoxically, this most private planet rules our relationship to the public, so many people with fourth house Moons also have a knack for connecting with the masses. After all, who doesn't hunger for the imaginative psychic awareness, the emotionally rich depth and the nurturing and healing companionship the Moon offers? We all crave the Moon's Soul food, which you can readily dish up and serve, if you are so inclined. What you are psychically hungry for, what most nourishes and satisfies your Soul, is something you can readily give others.

Comedienne, LGBT activist and talk show host Ellen De Generes' Moon is in the fourth house (Aries). Ellen's talk show has been a platform for collective healing, by featuring feel-good, humanitarian stories with inclusive agendas. Her loony, fun nature and warm-hearted generosity has endeared her to the public. Her home life is clearly a priority for her. She shares her home, a ranch, with many four-legged creatures and her partner, Portia.

You, too, may be very much out in the world, playing an active role in your greater community with your healing Moon. And when you look inward and seek your own counsel, heed your own intuition and honor your deep feeling-nature, a whole world opens up. You may ultimately find that you are most fulfilled living "inside here": whether noodling around your land, spending time with your four-legged friends, these private, quiet activities are about *going inside*—and that's where you find real happiness.

Your Soul Mate(s) and Tribe

In the fourth house, the Moon is in its natural domain—absolutely at home. Rooting, finding a partner and tribe to share your life with, is an undeniable and familiar call, deep in your Soul. To be happy, you need to establish a physical home, put down roots with your familiars. And to be happy, you must feel at home in, and psychologically familiar with, your feeling nature.

Likewise, you ask for the same emotional transparency from your partners. It's impossible for you to feel at home with those who can't be vulnerable with you, melt and openly surrender to the healing power of both laughter and tears. There's a fine balance to be struck here. You need a nurturing, emotionally self-aware, sensitive companion. Not someone who overdoes the emotional aspect of the relationship, nor one who doesn't express their emotions at all. Both are equally destabilizing for you. A partner doesn't need to be your emotional rock, because that would deny you your ability to be that for yourself, but neither do they need to be too emotionally soggy.

Many people aren't comfortable with *feeling*. By nature, feelings are irrational, complex, unstable and therefore risky. We aren't taught emotional skills. What should we do with anger? What about feelings of blame or vulnerability? These questions usually get lived and sorted in the fray of life, and our relationships, often with casualties. While emotional sophistication isn't everyone's forte, it is yours—or at least one you are majoring in in this lifetime. Feelings are the portal to your deep self. There are no shortcuts—at least not without denying yourself the pleasure of your own company.

The Moon needs to let down its guard to feel totally comfortable. La Luna needs to feel she can get loony and goofy. In fact, that's a sign that she trusts you as a clan member. You won't feel safe, loved and free with your Soul tribe unless you can be silly with them. Silliness is an underappreciated healing art form. Likewise, dorkiness, nerdiness, and just plain messing around. You want your tribe to be a little dorky or silly. You want them to "get you"!

Your silliness levels around others say oodles about who you call your family. It is a litmus test for your soulmates. Those you love will know your love is true by your comfort and willingness to share your oddball goofiness with them. Notice how comfortable you feel just being you, how at home you feel in sharing details about yourself around certain people. This is a real sign that you have found your person, and your tribe.

Likewise, people who take themselves too seriously, who are overly rigid, be it about dirty jokes you appreciate, your taste in music or your whimsical, eccentric habits, need not apply. Judging, criticizing, moralizing, should-ing…these habits all go against the nature of the Moon, which is acceptance and love. "Reject nothing. Accept and love," says the Moon, "and ye will be healed."

There's No Place Like Om

Without having a place to hang your hat, you feel adrift emotionally. Buying a home at some point in your life could be highly beneficial for you, not as an investment but as a way of saying, "This place is mine. I feel safe, rooted and nurtured." You will eventually want to anchor into a place that instills these feelings in you.

You may even feel strongly connected to a piece of land, a particular culture, person or tribe; all might resonate to a past-life experience for you. Kinship roots run deep for you, and it makes sense that you would feel drawn toward places or people you've partnered with in the past.

You need a protective bubble, safe haven or womb to collapse into, to feel your true experience, and feel your feelings. A home will do this for you. Your emotional truths can bubble up in a rooted environment. Home gives you a sense of safety and security to feel your feelings without censure, to arise organically, be unconditionally felt, accepted and released. And home is a place to re-fill your well with Soul satisfying activities that bring you happiness. If you're a gardener, the joy of turning your lawn into a botanical garden will bring you deep satisfaction. If you're a songwriter, this is where you unfurl your inner voice, dream, create and fantasize. At home, give your imagination permission to run wild. The mythic realm belongs to the Moon, and you have a taproot into this colorful and fantastic world.

The physical dwelling place you call home may resemble a nostalgic childhood one, or a piece of land you are called to cultivate, but above all it must have heart. Animals and pets easily bring heart. So, too, will two-legged companions who know how to let down their guard at the end of the day, who aren't afraid to be vulnerable and who are too wise to ever want to truly grow up and lose touch with the enchanting world of imagination!

Your quiet kid could be: a heart healer, empathic companion, true blue friend, poet, true romantic, crazy-silly, little caretaker, going for sainthood.

Your fourth house familiars are: emotionally available, feeling-oriented, sensitive, probably a little loony—they just make you laugh.

Your fourth house familiars are not: emotionally cool and distant, overly rigid, weighed down with glaring unhealed wounds, emotionally illiterate.

Ancestral healing: release ancestral blockages around the sharing of emotions and vulnerability. Someone in your lineage may have been emotionally or mentally unstable (luna-cy). Heal this by establishing an internal safe space for feeling your feelings, no matter how intense.

Your hidden treasure: we love the way your very being telepaths the message, "You're safe with me, you can cry on my shoulder." Honor this in yourself. Meditate on the healer you are, and have always been, since before you were born. Yes, you were the kid who found, and rescued, the bird with the broken wing. You sat at the lunch table with the unpopular friend when no one else would. You are a powerful healer. Let that out, let it shine.

Mercury in the Fourth House, or Virgo/Gemini on the Cusp:

The Intuitive Conversationalist

Angelique's doors were always open, and this was by design. Friends and neighbors knew they could stop by Angelique's for a cup of coffee, to borrow a cup of sugar or have a heart to heart about just about anything. She had grown up in a busy household where good conversation was always welcomed, and happiness was in a large measure tied to the comings and goings, and reported day-to-day experiences of her extended Latino family. She remembered being fascinated by the lives of her brothers and sisters, cousins, aunts, uncles—who brought their adventures and ideas, from politics to daily endeavors and travel to the family dinner table every night. Her childhood home was engaging, lively, bustling with stimulation.

If you have Mercury in the fourth house, you have a Soul need to experience an ongoing dialogue of exchange, learning and ideas with your Soul tribe, and at home. An environment with teachers, historians, crafts-persons or book lovers would fit the bill, as would a home life featuring travel or being constantly on the move. Your need to stay in motion, intellectually, and sometimes geographically, is likely rooted in reaction to a prior, or current, life dynamic of: lack of stimulation, not being free to follow one's curiosity, narrow-mindedness from members of your Soul tribe and partner.

Now, today, boredom and rigidity-in one's people or person is practically intolerable for you! Mercury is the planet in charge of our minds, of learning, information and communication. The first rule of thumb with Mercury here is: *Thou shalt not be bored at home.* The second rule of thumb is: *Thou shalt not be partnered to inflexible or rigid Soul mates.*

Curiosity, study, mental inquisitiveness, conversation need to be stoked by home and hearth fires. Change is not something to be avoided, but embraced, as are new ideas and experiences. Intellectual exploration and following your curiosity where it may lead are not optional, but required learning for you. A home life, and partner, that supports your need for education, movement and exchange furthers this. Continuing to learn and grow, through new ideas, people, experiences, supports the foundation of your very being. Altogether, these keep you feeling youthful and alive!

Restore and Renew

Some recharge their batteries by unplugging; others recharge through plugging in. You are more likely to fall into the latter category, because you do require a level of mental stimulation and conversation to feel connected and centered. In fact, the more often you are exposed to new ideas, things and people that make you go *hmmm*, *umm*, and *wow*, the younger you tend to feel. Bottom line: if you're not feeling engaged and stimulated in your own life, you don't feel as sparkly, youthful and alive as you could.

How will you keep the conduit of fresh, novel, interesting and different flowing in your life? Learning anything new, books and book groups, debates, discussions about current events, the going-ons about town and people you care for are a few of Mercury's favorite things. You feel at home exploring your varied interests. Yet you do need to "unplug" when your mind won't turn off, as will happen from time to time. Depending on the rest of your chart, overstimulation can be a real potential, even though few find constant mental stimulation and learning as grounding as you do.

Bill Gates shares this Mercury (Libra) placement with you. His parents were an academic and a lawyer, which meant Bill's intellectual and academic pursuits would be supported. He went to Harvard, but dropped out. Deciding computers would be the wave of the future, he devoted all of his time to creating a company called Microsoft. Not one to rest on his laurels, he has said that his vacations are

80

"think weeks" and that he hasn't taken a day off in thirteen years. You may identify with Gates' early focus on education, and maybe even your own brand of vision, business mindedness and ingenuity. Equally likely: the opposite. When younger, you may have not had your mind and curiosity encouraged and nourished to the extent you needed. Now it's time to tend the soil of your mind and imagination. One's mind, similar to a garden, must be cultivated, watered and nourished with a variety of interests, curiosities and passions; this remedies the dreaded experience of stagnation, which you are moving away from.

Don't underestimate your intelligence. A few words about intelligence: for some with this placement, intellectual agency can be overly valued or coveted by the family to the point of elitism. This can give rise to feelings of intellectual inadequacy, due to a lack of opportunity for higher education or not having one's ideas and voice heard or validated. Yet none are a true reflection of intelligence. In Greek myth, the God Mercury's intelligence was never linked to degrees, but his cleverness, dexterity, his adaptability to materialize what was needed in any given moment.

Mercury fourth house people have ingenuity and resourcefulness, displaying a real knack for pulling a rabbit from a hat when needed. Being in uncertain situations that require quick thinking and fancy footwork, be it a heated discussion at the dinner table, or changeable circumstances or situations with an unknowable outcome—like suddenly finding oneself a single parent who needs to figure out how to survive and thrive—bring on the inventiveness, creativity and multifaceted ingenuity of your fourth house Mercury. Thinking on your feet, improvising creative solutions "in the moment"? That's when your Mercury placement really shines.

Your Soul Mate(s) and Tribe

Mercury is the planet of brothers, sisters and neighborhoods-y type folks. The people who shaped you, and who you feel most deeply bonded to, may feel like, or actually be, biological brothers or sisters to you. Or you may find you have many "brothers or sisters from another mother." It gets really interesting when you've partnered up with, or married, someone who feels more like a sibling to you!

Your people, those who feel like home to you, are open-minded, naturally curious and non-dogmatic in their approach to life and beliefs. You might discover just how important this is to you when you partner with a person from a different cultural, ideological or religious background. For instance, to a South African, a Scandinavian person's thinking may be frustratingly inflexible and unyielding. So, if your partner is Scandinavian and you are from South Africa…there's a puzzle that could arrive you at an impasse.

While those who do not share your viewpoints are welcome to share a lively debate, those who are overly attached to their own point of view will prove too frustrating for you. Open-mindedness is that big of a value for you, in life and love. If someone doesn't share your beliefs, it could work, but if they aren't genuinely interested in you, curious about what makes you tick, open to discussing anything and everything, romance is a nonstarter.

In relationship, Mercury is quick to spot dis-ingeniousness; like pretending to be listening while "tuning out," boredom or feigning interest when disinterest is apparent. Nothing kills the romance for you like boredom—on either side. Your fourth house Mercury wedding vow is, "I will love, honor and *listen* to you with rapt attention and genuine interest." If one cannot offer you the same as you offer them, they are simply not your people.

In a nutshell, your meeting of the minds must not only include your minds, but your hearts and your erotic body(s). While mental chemistry should be at the top of your list for a life-mate, you are more than a walking brain. Genuine interest in, open-mindedness and an attitude of playful curiosity toward each other are like foreplay before the main course, allowing for the heart to fully open to love. That is the deeper message of fourth house Mercury energy.

There's No Place Like Om

There's a seeming contradiction with this placement; while the fourth house is innately oriented toward introversion, quiet and privacy, Mercury is not. Mercury is a lively and engaging planet that prefers interaction and sociability. You may feel at home living communally, with roommates. You may be at home in a busy co-op living arrangement, an apartment building with many neighbors, or an urban environment versus a rural one. Or you may feel at home in an environment surrounded with books, have a huge library in your house or live in a stimulating, youthful university town.

Imagine a home with a revolving door, the kind that allows people to come in and out. While conversation, debate and foot traffic are welcomed in this environment, to prevent burnout or overload, an open-door policy is balanced by needs for privacy, periods of conversation and stimulation with periods of quiet time (these needs vary depending on whether the rest of the chart is primarily an introverted or extroverted one). Any planet in the fourth house needs its privacy protected. You need a place in your home, a workspace perhaps, where you can retreat into your mind, alone.

While you can entertain yourself for hours alone, you often prefer the company of intelligent, youthful compatriots. They need not be young; youthfulness, like maturity, is not dependent on age but an attitude of lively vivacity and sparkle. As anyone with half a Mercury knows, you only truly grow old when you've become unwilling to try new things. Stop listening to new music, eating new foods, entertaining new ideas, and that's when old age sets in. An engaging listener with a twinkle in their eye, a spring in their step, a clever quip on their tongue and who is willing to try that new Pakistani restaurant? That's your life mate, your people, your Soul tribe.

Your quiet kid could be: a clever student, curious George, little talker, little networker, fibber, sprite, fairy or elemental.

Your fourth house familiars are: interesting, curious, open-minded, lively, effervescent and youthful in both mind and spirit.

Your fourth house familiars are not: dogmatic, narrow-minded, boring, pretending to listen when they're really making their grocery list.

Ancestral healing: release ancestral blockages around the new and different. Someone in your lineage may've been threatened by undefined, fluid expressions of identity concepts and ideas. Heal this by being willing to experiment and letting go of preconceptions, opinions and judgments. Embrace your curious nature. Vow to be open-minded, without requiring it from those who cannot. Don't let others closed minds drag you down.

Your hidden treasure: you have something relevant to say and/or share, probably both, so as fun as it is to stay in that mind of yours, remember to bring your ideas out into the world occasionally. Your ability to improvise conversationally and situationally, connect to others and form networks ensures that you will never be left hanging on your own. And never forget the curious imp you were as a kid, who had all kinds of crazy and brilliant ideas. She/he's still in there! Imagine what kind of (good) trouble you could get into if you allowed those beautiful ideas of yours to take full flight.

Venus in the Fourth House, or Taurus/Libra on the Cusp: The Sensitive Companion

Everyone wanted to be invited to Riley's house for dinner. With an art collection rivaling Gertrude Stein's and great taste in music and décor, she was a sophisticated hostess. When Riley decided you were part of the family, she would do anything for you. Kind, empathetic and extremely tuned into the desires of others', she had always been that way—though those who were not invited into her inner circle may never know her in this way. To those who didn't know her well, Riley could appear self-reliant, aloof even. Yet she had sensitive and aesthetic responses to her environment and to the people around her. On the outside, she could be tough as nails, but inside, she was as sensitive as an ice cream cone to the sun on a hot summer's day.

Family was important to Riley. She often found herself in the role of peacemaker, negotiating sibling or parental relationships with the ease of a seasoned counselor. This wasn't necessarily by choice. It was a skill, a way of surviving in an early childhood family dynamic that was far from peaceful. If there were a way to make an intolerable situation a little easier on everyone, she could be that buffer, though often at a cost to her own peace.

If you were born with Venus in the area of the birth chart aligned with your deepest sense of self, you feel yourself to be deeply Venusian—which is to say you are far more sensitive to balance, beauty and harmony in both your relationships and your immediate environment than you may let on! You might find yourself creating a beautiful home, because it fills you with a sense of peace. You may wile away the hours on crafts websites, or spend your time arranging flowers, playing with interior decorating apps, or painting, because these are relaxing and nurturing activities for you. Venus is the archetype of the artist, among other things. Whether or not you identify as an artist, you have a knack for creating harmony and peaceful order among people, things, ideas, situations.

In prior lives, or in this one, Venusian concerns like social appropriateness, sensitivity to others' opinions, focus on appearances or "how things look" took up too much emotional real estate in your family. Equally possible, social awareness and appropriateness could've been altogether missing in your childhood, forcing you to compensate for others' lack of sensitivity and social tone deafness with deference, tact, grace, sensitivity - qualities you have in spades.

However, smoothing over others' rough spots with your very being can become a way of life. And this role you played in early life may have injured your trust that others will love you, not for who they want you to be, but for who you truly are. You move forward and heal by addressing those unhealthy relationship patterns that once worked to help you survive your childhood, but are no longer required of, nor fulfilling for, you. Authentic relationships aren't about being nice, pleasing or how anyone looks on paper, but having one's true self joyously, mutually honored. That's when you know you are healed and free to love and to be loved.

Restore and Renew

With Venus here, you draw from the wellspring of the Goddess, Venus. Creativity, joy, pleasure and ultimately giving yourself permission to do things that make you happy are essential. With Venus at the bedrock of your very existence, her magic woven into the substructure of your imaginative psyche, Venus worship can be pursued with abandon. You truly have no excuse to deny yourself pleasure! Buy yourself flowers for no reason…celebrate Friday with champagne, because it's Venus-day…or whip up a love spell for yourself… Anytime you unabashedly pursue recreational, artistic and creative interests, even if in the privacy of your own mind and home, you honor your need for toe-curling titillations and decadent delights.

Take your pleasure in quiet, introspective and solitary ways, and you truly honor the need of a more private, retiring fourth house Venus.

In myth, Venus was a social Goddess, yet the fourth house is quieter, more reflective. Creative outlets that can be pursued alone are rewarding for you. Whether you paint, draw or write, art can entirely transform your perceptions, let alone your entire life. Louisa May Alcott, author of the book *Little Women*, among others, had Venus in Capricorn in her fourth house. Though raised in and limited by extreme poverty, she wrote books about a kinder, gentler, gentile life and populated them with characters from her own experiences. By the time she died, she had created a fortune and legacy. She magically wrote herself into the abundant life she had crafted! True artists always transform something base, neglected, un-liked or unwanted into something beautiful and true. Though she got a lot of play for her abilities to enchant lovers, that's the actual magic Venus had up her girdle.

Speaking of Venus magic, the law of attraction is a form of Venus magic, which at essence is about aligning with what and who turns you on (and when you truly do this, what and who you don't will eventually go away). Discerning and honoring what you like and enjoy, and who you like and enjoy, has far-reaching consequences. You literally, albeit often unconsciously, have attractive magnetism— for good or ill. For instance, when you allow a chaotic, wounded relationship into your innermost circle, you also bring chaos into your reality, and this will always diminish your ability to experience joy and peace. When you decide you only want to be around people who feel good to you, you feel harmonious, peaceful, blissful.

Yes, some people have real issues, and you're not writing those people off. It's more of an energetic law of resonance, which, if you can depersonalize, you vibrate with at your core. Some people will resonate with you, and others will not, and those people will make you feel crazy, or much worse. In your childhood, you probably learned to make up for what others lacked, to be the buffer when everything got bumpy around you, and accept a level of crazy as normal. Yet as an adult, you don't have to do that. The decision to not be around people who do not peacefully resonate with you does not make you insensitive or unkind. Actually, your deep sensitivity to others means you, more than most, must learn to honor who and what resonates with you—and who and what does not.

Your Soul Mate(s) and Tribe

In astrology, Venus is everyone's darling; everyone loves Venus! Niceness and champagne kisses, peaches and cream, what's not to love? But herein lies the problem. Artifice, pleasantries, even money, can be like someone wearing heavy perfume on a hot day in the subway—it distracts but doesn't hide the stink. Family has been known to hide their dirty laundry behind social appropriateness and smiles, to manipulate others through loyalty or obligation and call that "love." Karmically, it is likely that you have sustained some injuries through a particular kind of deception, one that wears a smiling, appearance-conscious face…and is far from the honest truth.

Was your family really as perfect as some members like to paint them to be? Due to Venus' tendency to gild the crap truth with fancy frosting, it's always a good idea to question whether your family life was so idyllic and spotless as everyone (or you) paints it out to be—especially if you're having trouble creating a family and roots of your own. An inability to form lasting attachments to a new Soul tribe may be traced to old fourth house issues, so examine any idealizations of home life, or family bonds, you have. Patterns of behavior can be inherited here, so look to family members for common threads of unhappiness, heartbreak, abandonment, rejection and explore those and how they might similarly play out in your own life (learn more about ancestral healing in section four, in the chapter *Venus therapy*).

Trust is all-important for you in relationship. What inspires your trust and confidence in another? Is it caring and compassion? Openness and authenticity? Sometimes we form false values that aren't really our own, because they are more socially acceptable ones. We believe we need a life partner who is a reliable steady Eddy, but that's a reaction against the chaotic upbringing we experienced. Or we esteem provider-ship and social status in a partner at the cost of emotional support. Perhaps we value loyalty, or being agreeable, at the cost of being truthful, and then when the truth comes out we feel betrayed. We may learn about what does or doesn't inspire our trust the hard way. The success of your chosen family hinges on your self-awareness; understanding both what truly undermines your confidence in relationship and what supports it.

Venus is the Goddess of harmony, connection and discernment. Learning how to choose who your right people are is a necessary function for aligning with those you love. One thing is certain: Soul mates who are worthy of your trust will be as democratic with you as you are with them. They will give your happiness as much weight as they give their own. They will not ask you to do anything you wouldn't feel fine also asking of them. In real love, no one sacrifices or compromises their self for another's life path or decisions…and if you are told otherwise, run, don't walk, in the other direction!

There's No Place Like Om

Your ideal abode will be part healing sanctuary and part artist's getaway, a place where you can retreat into peaceful relaxation with your partner, and take creative down time. Since your home environment is a generative energy source for harmony, beauty and peace, why not make it beautiful and lovely? When you're feeling funky or off, retreating to a sanctuary that reflects your aesthetics and tastes is the number one thing you can do to lift your emotional vibration. Turn on music while making dinner, read poetry by the fire…you can always create the mood for joy and calm to find you.

The energetics and aesthetics of our home environment is an underappreciated source of well-being—and one we can influence. Do you like lots of light in your home? Windows? Mirrors? Crystals and gemstones? The sound of trickling water? Aphrodite/Venus loves shiny things, reflective surfaces and objects. She was born from the sea, so has an affinity with water and ocean themes. Your taste will be individual. Honoring your unique preferences, taste and intuition around design and environment insures magical harmony in your home. You might also enjoy Feng Shui, which creates balance and harmony through sensitive, artful placement.

The most important question of all: what do you love about your home? As with the phrase "beauty is in the eye of the beholder," the most beautiful space in the world is the one that you love to be in. It will uplift your spirit, soothe your Soul, center your emotions and enhance your overall sense of connection to yourself. So be artful. Indulge your love for design. Surround yourself with your signature style. The people you love will respect the gift you have for creating a calm, relaxing and elegant living environment.

Finally, a low-stress, low-drama committed relationship with a Venusian partner heals your trust and offers you deep security. Your ideal marital or committed partner is Venusian, like you. Venus people have natural courtesy, charm and tact, are relationship-oriented and sensitive toward what others want and need. In other words, no more one-way streets or compromises that leave you feeling put off; they will be just as empathic and sensitive toward you as you are toward them! How will you recognize these considerate and charming people with whom you are deeply bonded? From the deep energetic sense of relaxation and peace you feel when you are with them. You simply find yourself going *ahhhhh…* in their presence.

Your quiet kid could be: a little diplomat, sensitive artist, people pleaser, easygoing playmate, little judge, mediator, beauty queen.

Your fourth house familiars are: mutually honoring, appreciative, gracious, tactful, easygoing, a pleasure to be around.

Your fourth house familiars are not: superficial, materialistic, autocratic, crass, rude, addicted to drama, sort of embarrassing to be around.

Ancestral healing: release ancestral blockages around love, authenticity and trust. Someone in your lineage may've chosen money and security over love, the illusion of a perfect relationship over a mutually honoring one, or the artifice of keeping up appearances— wanting family members to appear or look perfect for the status quo, stifling authenticity and trust. All of the above can be very damaging to the family. Heal this by placing trust in the love you give yourself and acting from the values that you, and you alone, form (not values others create for you). Understanding your ancestral inheritance, the good and ugly, is key in forming permanent intimate bonds.

Your hidden treasure: you are a deeply sensitive relationship artist, a gifted seduction vixen, and you have more power in Venus realms than you probably give yourself credit for! Own your ability to facilitate joy, beauty and harmony, be gloriously magnetic, express yourself with tact and charm. Drop old habits of deferring to others' joys and happiness before claiming your own; take your pleasure first. Master the intuitive art of giving to others, not to please them, but to get what it is *you both* most desire. Understand that your personal law of attraction rests entirely in how you consciously embody your magnetism and Venus energy. Own it, own it, own it. When it comes to Venus, self-possession is 9/10 of the law.

Mars in the Fourth House, or Aries on the Cusp:

The Soulful Warrior

Ani grew up in war-torn Bosnia during the 1990s. Going to sleep to the sound of gunfire was an all too familiar uncomfortable childhood memory for Ani, who remembers nights of covering the windows with black sheets to keep snipers from targeting their little village.

Though she immigrated to Austria long ago, Ani's memories of the violence in her homeland remain, although no one close to her knows of her childhood scars, her personal history. She doesn't think about that time of life very often anymore, but deep down she can feel how those experiences shaped her. Her upbringing turned her into a survivor and a warrior. Today, Ani is co-owner of a design firm in a competitive office environment. Weaned on the milk of courage in the face of fear, she is a courageous risk-taker and leader in her professional life, and is the only woman in a male dominated office. Yet terror still occasionally appears in nighttime dreams, she wakes up with a racing heart, fearing for her life and that of her family's. Her childhood has left an invisible mark of violence on her Soul.

Your story may not be as extreme as Ani's, but deep down, your Soul, too, carries the mark of Mars, God of War. In past lives, or in this one, you, too, may've become a survivor at a young age, raised in a war-like environment, faced a family member's violence or rage, been the target of aggression. You may have needed to defend or protect your family from harm. Whatever the case, a lingering feeling remains—the feeling that you may need to drop everything to protect loved ones, or protect yourself. Alternately, in childhood you may've felt like you got lost in the shuffle of your family's survival needs, so you needed to work harder to assert yourself, to get what you needed.

Mars energy has sharp edges. Yet just as it takes practice to build up a muscle, when we squarely face and work with conflict, we feel stronger for it. You'll have the opportunity: your closest mates will bring out your heat! They will activate your passions, your deepest desires, and your ability to set an example for others. They may ask you to be the leader *in your relationship with them*, even as you question your ability to do that. They may consciously or unconsciously ask you to step up to the plate when a difficult situation requires it. They will make you angry. They will challenge you. Guaranteed, if you have any buttons to push around right use of anger, boundaries, individuality and autonomy, they will find those buttons and push them! In so doing, they show you how to wisely use your strength. Just as a warrior can only discover his or her skills when tested, this is how your Soul's mates help reveal to you who you truly are.

Restore and Renew

Where Mars is located its non-stop action, so you may find home and family to be less of a place of retreat and refuge, and more of a place of constant activity, compelling needs, projects and beloved people that demand your attention. Since Mars is the planet of energy (and anger and self-assertion), you expend a lot of physical energy in this area, which actually suits you. Nothing's more relaxing than being called to action to help a family member in need, or be able to move a longstanding project, interest, off your plate. Yet you may wonder if it is possible for you to take a day off for rest. We all need it, even those who need less rest and retreat time than others. You just may need to be very intentional about slowing down your pace for rest.

Since home, typically a place of privacy and retreat, is so busy and demanding for you, well-developed boundaries are necessary. People will impinge on your time, all the time, when you allow them to do so. If this sounds like you, consider this is in large part because you have a naturally heightened habit of believing that the world will fall apart without you. When we anticipate emergencies, whether or not those emergencies are real (and 99.9% of the time they are not actually emergencies), we tend to make ourselves available to every little crisis on the radar. You may complain about how busy everything is, but deep down you may really like it and want to be in high demand. Similar to an email inbox that will just keep filling up so you can never quite seem to get ahead, this happens because you are willing and able to take it on. If you weren't willing and able, no emails!

No matter whether you secretly enjoy feeling indispensable or not, at times you do wish you could just hand over the reins to someone else. Just do it! Remember, no one will fall apart without you. Taking the time away to do activities, selfishly—that is, things you enjoy, activities just for you—allows you to take back your focus from others' needs, and restores your energy back to you. Leave the family to fend for themselves for the night and go to dinner with friends. Have a regular date with the gym, or any physical activity that allows you to let off steam, move energy, and simply be in your own space. Prioritize your needs; no one can manage or be in charge of your energy but you. In your closest Soul mate relationships, your rule of thumb should be, there can be no "we" without a "me" first. Claim "me time."

Your Soul Mate(s) and Tribe

Intimacy is not just flowers, moonlit walks and romance—although they are certainly a prerequisite to it (and keeping long-term relationships glowing). Intimacy is also an arena where we get to work on healing old habits of misunderstanding and conditioning. With Mars here, you may feel a particular kind of vulnerability to your partner: They could love you, they could hurt you, they could betray, abandon or leave you. Those risks are certainly somewhat real, as every person who has ever fallen in love knows. Intimacy is inherently risky. After all, people are mysterious, least of all to ourselves! Even after decades together, many couples acknowledge they are still discovering new things about their partners.

The awareness that we are most vulnerable to those whom we most love is hardwired into our human DNA, too. When we care so deeply about someone it means they have the capacity to trigger our most primal caveman or cavewoman feelings of jealousy, anger, hurt, pain. If we didn't care, they wouldn't have the ability to trigger us.

Yet many of your intimate vulnerabilities and fears are just shadows, an exaggerated play of perception leftover from a time long ago when you felt, or indeed were, abandoned, hurt and betrayed. Like a phantom limb that acts up when an insecurity is triggered, or a similar energy draws near, defensiveness and anger are warning signs that you are retracing old steps, revisiting an old battlefield of fear.

In partnership, conflict will arise. Remember, this is Mars. You are learning lessons around fighting fairly, boundaries, being in high heat situations and working it out, together. Your partner gets your blood boiling. On the flip side, they also get your blood going, in a sexy way! Yet, for the kind of fight that makes tempers flare and voices rise to a fever pitch, the only water for that heat is the humble admittance, *I am afraid.* Afraid of abandonment, rejection, pain. The more ferocious anger looks, feels, sounds, the stronger the fear. Take time to sit with what arises, commit to honestly feel what comes up for you during those high heat moments. That's how you heal.

You fare best with a partner who has a relatively healthy relationship to their expression of anger, that is, one who is equally able to feel and exchange their heat with you *without blaming, getting nasty, abusive or pinning their shortcomings onto you.* Beware: the wounded warrior who blames, is passive aggressive or has issues with rage. That would be a huge red light, to re-evaluate how you want to be treated. Ultimately, people can only treat you in the way you allow them to.

Here's the takeaway for you: having Mars in the fourth house will generate sexy heat in your Soul mate relationships, and the ongoing facing of hot topics that might make another run for cover. But not you! You are built for this. Think about two warriors holding a pow-wow, or important discussion. A great warrior like you deserves another capable equal for a mate. Even, and especially, under the most pressured, stressful circumstances. After all, that's when everyone's true colors show for what they really are.

When you find the one who is equally fierce as they are tender, who is as honest and forthright as they are caring and kind, who loves your warrior strength and power without feeling threatened by it, watch out! They just might melt your armor…along with your heart.

There's No Place Like Om

Independence is sought at home. You require the freedom to do your own thing, be it creative projects, working on your professional interests or building and remodeling your home—this may be a real possibility, as Mars rules physical brute strength and it gives you the chance to flex yours. Freedom and initiative to take the time to do what you need to do to feel good, strong and take care of yourself is central to avoiding the power struggles that Mars can invite when you do not honor your own will, needs, feelings and desires.

With an on-the-go-and-all-fired-up Mars, what will make your home life feel peaceful? Have a room or office to call your own. Create boundaries of time around when and how you are available to family members who need you. Take space when you need. Simply honoring the reality that, even—and perhaps especially more so— when coupled, two people must have independent lives, apart from their partner and family, helps. Establish this understanding at your relationship's start and you will save so much lost time spent in arguments that arise from too much socially enforced togetherness.

Home matters will consistently stimulate your warrior spirit. Just knowing this about yourself can help you to respect what arises as normal, and as an invitation to work on your Mars issues. If you shut down during conflict, when conflict arises, set the intention to take a deep breath, ground your energy, and use your voice. If anger is a hotspot, an area that is hard for you to express, set the intention to not bury your anger. Swing an axe, get out a hammer and some nails and just hit that wood. Vow to be straightforward with others about what you want and need. Vow to honor your personal needs and desires at home and with family. *Your inner warrior*—his or her anger, fear and honesty—*deserves your respect.* Honor your warrior!

Every warrior needs a safe place to retire to, someplace private where you don't need to feel on guard. You may be attracted to homes with high desert walls, or a home perched on a mountaintop lookout with a bird's-eye view of potential intruders or invaders! Your home need not be a fortress. True security has no need for defenses, fences or barriers; security only comes from being in right relation to yourself.

When you trust yourself to be true to your desires, needs, wants and feelings, no matter how edgy and prickly they feel, or how unpopular they are with others, you gain a powerful foundation of security that cannot ever come from anything external to you. That's when you become the invincible warrior Soul you were born to be.

Your quiet kid could be: a little warrior, the family hero, a super-defender and protector of underdogs, honest Abe, impulsive, quite the daredevil.

Your fourth house familiars are: honest, straightforward, independent, have healthy respect for and relationship to anger, know how to ask for what they want and need—and aren't threatened by the same in you.

Your fourth house familiars are not: rageaholics, violent, coarse, passive aggressive, addicted to blaming others, rage or adrenaline.

Ancestral healing: release ancestral conditioning around expression of anger, rage, sexual heat, honesty. Someone in your lineage may've over-expressed, or conversely under-expressed, their heat, sexuality and anger. It's up to you to heal this, or you attract that pattern in partners. Heal through allowing this hot energy to safely release in your feeling body. Respect your anger. Learn to fight fairly. Risk honesty with those you love; the more honest you are about your experience, the safer, more loved and supported you will feel. Create space for autonomy and healthy boundaries in intimacy and with family; not standing up for yourself, not respecting your own autonomy is the fastest path to resentment in relationship.

Your hidden treasure: what's in your secret arsenal? Soulful honesty and fearless leadership. In stress and duress, you know what must be done, and so you get it done, making you the warrior everyone wants on their home team. Likewise, when it's time to cut through the b.s., and get at the truth of the matter, you're one hundred percent there. Only those who know you well may know the loyal, soulful warrior inside you, but it's always there. When the pressure is turned up and on, your instincts serve you in any situation requiring courage, leadership and split-second decision making.

Jupiter in the Fourth House, or Sagittarius on the Cusp: The Visionary Soul

From external appearances, Heather hadn't had an easy early life, but she was blessed with a wellspring of optimism and a deep sense of faith in life. When circumstances made life seem quite grim, she always looked for the silver lining, and if she couldn't see it, she trusted that one would soon appear. As a result, as the years passed, she increasingly became what others would call "lucky." She became upwardly mobile through her partner, married into a large family and lived in a home on a hill with a panoramic view that made her feel inwardly spacious and amazingly blessed. Others saw Heather as lucky to have such a good life, but it hadn't always been that way. She didn't settle for less; if life showed her less, she knew it was temporary. Heather had faith in the generosity of life. She felt this deep within her Soul…and so this would only lead to good things.

Jupiter is the planet of expansion, generosity, faith, perspective. In the private fourth house, Jupiter is tucked away in a hidden garden. You may not consider yourself a spiritual person (or you may), but dig deeper and you really do have a despite-all-odds type of abiding faith in the goodness and generosity of life. The more in touch you are with this deep faith inside yourself, the more likely you are to externalize it as a reality in your own life. You don't have to be a "true believer"—in yourself, in life or anything—to reap Jupiter's blessings (though it infinitely helps); Jupiter delivers, anyhow, since faith, blessed-ness and generosity are its energetic calling card.

With Jupiter here, your karma is to experience the domestic realm of family, marriage, hearth and home as an expansive and generous in all ways—spiritually, materially, emotionally—experience. This may be in a prior (or this) life reaction to having exactly the opposite

99

experience! Your family of origin may've been a nightmare for you, or conversely, a blessing. Regardless, you are carrying good karma surrounding family and domesticity forward into today. No matter your circumstances, since the fourth house is naturally associated with retirement generally, as time goes on, life only gets better.

One adage remains consistently true, though, where we find Jupiter; if you want to touch the stars, you must reach for them. On all matters related to settling down and finding my true home and family, consistently be more Jupiterian about it all—that is, aim high, and believe you deserve what you want. It may take a few shots, but set your intentional arrow. Jupiter was an expert marksman!

Restore and Renew

Imagine seeing a sparkling oasis in the middle of the desert. You have been traveling long and are bone-tired weary. You have been thirsty for so many days. Now, you are greeted warmly, offered food, comfort, drink, some entertainment of poetry and Sufi dancing. Within a matter of minutes, your memories of being cold, alone and hungry for weeks entirely vanish, replaced by firelight's glow, a full belly and the feeling that everything is okay…and always will be.

Life is long. It can be traumatic, and it can be a grind. Many people barely survive the slings and arrows of true hardship, let alone the daily survival demands of work, family, culture. Living can take its toll. Jupiter says, "I see it's been a long road for you, weary traveler. Take off your sandals, dip your toes in this water, drink some of my wine, eat some food." Jupiter is naturally generous. And through receiving that generosity, Jupiter restores our faith in life.

Chances are, you've received this kind of surprising generosity at various points in your life. Where Jupiter appears in your birth chart, you will receive respite and renewal in whatever form you most need in order to feel in touch with life's inherent faith, possibility and magic again. In the fourth house, Jupiter weaves its generous magic through your home and family life. The million-dollar question is: *Do you have enough faith in life, and in yourself, to claim it?*

Periodically, your faith in family and home needs to be renewed and expanded upon. The missive with Jupiter is always to think and envision bigger things for yourself than you've previously thought possible. If you've always dreamt of living on a ranch or on a tropical island, it is within your reach…as long as you give yourself the permission to want it and the faith to have it. Perhaps you want to make a trip to your ancestral homelands but can't figure out a way to swing it, financially. *Give yourself permission to want it.* This is the trick with Jupiter, never underestimating what's possible for you.

What type of living situation makes you feel expansive? What would make you feel so blessed and lucky to come home to at the end of a bone-wearying day? With Jupiter in the fourth house, what makes you feel delightfully expansive also restores and renews your Soul. Perhaps you've dreamt of living in a house in the high desert with lots of four-legged friends you call family. Perhaps you dream of starting a spiritual retreat center in Costa Rica, or living abroad.

Jupiter is the generous abundance of life itself. You carry this expansive, faith-full, generous nature within your very Soul. If you can own this about yourself, you can call in anything you want.

Your Soul Mate(s) and Tribe

No Debbie Downers for you! Your intimate tribe members are naturally optimistic and your number one fans. They believe in you in ways you may find difficult, at times, to believe in yourself. They aren't blowing hot air up your you-know-what, either; they hold up the mirror to your true awesomeness so that you can more clearly see how amazingly gifted and wonderful in all ways you are.

It is vital that your long-term partners and life mates, your adopted family and chosen tribe, have an expansive, optimistic, generous and tolerant nature. They think big, and encourage you to do the same.

They may or may not be spiritual. They are definitely visionary. They are natural students of life; never assuming they have all the answers, they are happy in the search for them. They don't think or preach that there is only one right way to think, live or be (that is, they aren't afraid of things, people, places and ideas they don't understand).

Likewise, people who are dogmatic, unduly negative or attached to a narrow belief system will cramp your style and clip your wings—the very wings you need to expand in any direction you find authentic and true for you. This doesn't mean your chosen family and partners will always understand you, an impossible request. They will, however, understand the nature of human differences, and so will not be threatened by the ways you and they differ in perception, beliefs and understanding. In fact, some of your favorite moments together will be the ways you can expand one another's perspective on life by simply sharing your different perceptions.

In the karmic past, you may've been unduly restricted by your family of origin—by their beliefs, prejudices, harsh intolerances. Someone always made sure you knew there was a better, more right, more virtuous way, and they made sure to remind you of their self-importance! Now, your chosen family reminds you that the most important faith of all is faith in yourself. They give you the freedom to find out who you are, what you want, and put the wind underneath your wings so you can get there. They encourage you to do what is truly right for you, whatever that may be. *They believe in you.* Their belief in you could be exactly the drop of Jupiter you most need.

There's No Place Like Om

Make it big, exotic or overseas...whatever kind of home you imagine yourself flourishing in and wherever you choose to live, aim to feel expansive and rich. Jupiter's boon awaits. This is the place you get to experience feelings of blessedness, bounty and wealth in all of its forms. To get there, though, you will need to take a leap of faith.

Where we find Jupiter, we find the risk of not aiming high enough or underestimating what is possible for ourselves. In your case, this might look like: not investing in your home, not liking where you live geographically, being dismissive about the role your aesthetic tastes, preferences and desires have in making you feel "wealthy," being too financially frugal when it comes to where and how you want to live, or too utilitarian about decorating or enhancing your living space.

Jupiter is all about opening us up to myriad possibilities, yet it takes a leap to get there. Once you take a few risks—say, you spend a little more than you'd planned on that beautiful lamp made out of rose quartz, or you have a new deck installed in that same beautiful rich wood you saw when you were visiting Asia—you discover that every penny spent skyrockets your quality of life. Every morning, you take your coffee on that beautiful deck and dream of Asia. Every evening you sit under the glow of your rose quartz lamp and feel the love.

To those without Jupiter in the fourth house, paying a premium for the perfect cotton sheets or a marble top kitchen counter, when you love to cook, may be unnecessarily extravagant. For you, the enrichment this adds to your quality of life is priceless. To wake up every day in a space you love and feel so crazy lucky—this is living!

Lavish attention and care on your home. Take risks on enhancing your living space. Move. If you don't have to, don't cut corners on buying the furniture items, artworks, piece of land or home that make you feel opulent, wealthy and blessed…and you will be.

Your quiet kid could: be an adventure-lover, a gypsy, little philosopher, know-it-all, easily inspired, have more to offer the world than you might first think.

Your fourth house familiars are: optimistic, expansive, generous, fun-loving, tolerant, not afraid to think big and take calculated risks.

Your fourth house familiars are not: petty, puritanical, stern, miserly, intolerant know-it-alls who are afraid of things they don't understand.

Ancestral healing: release ancestral blockages around intolerance and judgment. Someone in your lineage was narrow minded, philosophically, morally or spiritually self-righteous, or failed to imbue the big picture of life with proper perspective, meaning and faith—which limited your tribe's ability to think more was possible. To heal this, envision a bigger, brighter future for yourself than the one you were shown, develop a meaningful philosophy of life that feels true for you, and take leaps of faith when it comes to creating your home and chosen family. Release the conditioning of self-judgment, negativity and intolerance and open to possibilities.

Your hidden treasure: in life, the leaps of faith required of you have mostly to do with taking a risk on what you have to offer. Chances are, your life experiences are more valuable, interesting and delightful than you might think! Instead of keeping them buried deep down inside, risk sharing yourself with the world. You can expand the perspectives of those you love by sharing a personal story, or advance culture by contributing your knowledge on a subject. Your ability to see possibilities where others may not, makes you a closet visionary, and as you find the faith to risk asking for more from yourself, and your life, you encourage others to do the same.

Saturn in the Fourth House, or Capricorn on the Cusp: The Committed Realist

Growing up, Kelly had everything she needed—three meals a day, shelter, care and protection, but she noticed something was missing. Her parents were hard-working and modest people who, despite putting on happy faces to the outside world, regular attendance at events and being generally well-regarded by their community, were not what you'd call happy. The atmosphere around the dinner table, even during celebrations like birthday parties, was a sobering experience for Kelly, a naturally fun-loving, happy and adventuresome kid. She never understood the dark cloud that seemed to hang over the household, until she became an adult and Kelly learned that her parents had grown up during the Great Depression. Even though they'd come out okay, it put a restrictive shadow on her experience, a depressive mood over the family home.

What does it feel like to be born with Saturn in the fourth house? What resources has it given you? With Saturn here, your inner mood is serious-minded, pragmatic and attuned to the hard, or more accurately, real difficult realities of life. Karmically, or in this lifetime, you may have lived in an early childhood home that was marked by limitation, depression or unhappiness of caregivers. The restrictive atmosphere may've forced you to grow up quickly, be more responsible at an early age than other kids. More family demands may've been asked of you. Perhaps you had to take care of siblings, do housework or be understanding of adult matters (finances, relationship troubles) before you were mature enough to do so.

As a result, you have developed strengths and skills. From your early life (and potentially lifetimes), you bring forward hard-won resilience. An "old Soul", you may've always felt older than your years. You are

105

capable of enduring periods of difficulty, hardship and limitation, responsible in ways others may not have the ability to be, resourceful, and generally okay with being alone for long stretches of time.

Life gives us many opportunities to step up to the plate when loved ones are in need, or when they simply do not have the ability to respond to a hard reality. You are built for these kinds of situations. When you decide to be there for others, you mean it. A vow, a commitment, is something you feel deep in your bones.

Yet just because you can doesn't mean you have to. You don't have to write your own ticket back into needful situations that foisted these abilities on you in the first place. If you make choices out of guilt, tether yourself to people who are needy, decide it's better to be alone than rely on others, settle for less and lack for too long…or any other situation that asks far too much endurance of you and not enough Soul nourishment, your strengths become a weakness. You and your well-developed, strong backbone can capably endure difficulty for a long time…but why make yourself do that?

Restore and Renew

Imagine, after a hard day's work, coming home to a house full of dirty dishes or messy home. Perhaps your house mate says they intend to do the dishes or clean up, but something always gets in the way of those "good intentions," and so you end up doing it. Every. Single. Night. *No big deal,* you tell yourself. What effect does that have on you over time? It's kind of like the analogy of a frog being slowly boiled alive; the frog doesn't realize he's about to boil to death because the water has been turned up too slowly to register.

Death by taking on too much responsibility, because you can, is a slow, voiceless death. It kills your free time, the time you'd spend taking care of yourself, devoting yourself to a hobby, pleasure or creative pursuit. It kills your sense of fair exchange, mutual respect and reciprocity. It kills your joy incrementally—one unwanted obligation at a time. This is the exact thing you want to watch out for with Saturn in the fourth house. Family commitments and domestic partnership can certainly foist self-sacrifice onto us. It's not unusual. Maybe because it is too easy to take on domestic gender roles, or fall into habits of convenience. Plus, modern life is demanding. But ultimately, when we take on commitments that we really, deep down, don't want to be doing, we abnegate our authority. In so doing, we set our self up for constant domestic drudgery, a joyless existence.

What might a better "coming home at the end of the day" look like for you? So that you can really and truly restore and renew yourself? Saturn needs its solitude and alone time—whether to work on a favorite project, zone out on Netflix, meditate or anything else. You restore yourself—your energy, your sanity, your psyche, your imagination—through taking time away from everyone and everything so that you can just be. Alone time is paramount for you; it is where you find quiet contentment within, in the stillness you can hear your Soul's yearnings. Claiming alone time needs to be a priority.

Secondly, setting realistic parameters and agreements for co-habitation and division of labor is one hundred percent reasonable for you. Who takes out the trash? Who pays the bills every month (on time)? Evaluate these questions, and re-negotiate regularly, if needed, to make sure the energy exchange is not imbalanced. If one person enjoys cooking, the other is responsible for dishes…and so on. Energy balance/imbalance is real. You feel it. If not consciously, in the way you will slowly, almost imperceptibly feel yourself becoming resentful, moody, miserable. Boiled alive.

Your Soul Mate(s) and Tribe

Since you are so competent and capable, you attract responsibilities on the homefront—from family and tribe members who need your strong backbone, your ability to do things that must get done but maybe no one else wants to do. Boundaries are vital for you.

The best of Saturn in the fourth house is your capacity for demonstrating inner strength, can-do and authority in all areas of your life, including domestic. This could look like custom building a home, one where you get to have a room of your own, a Saturn sanctuary for your work and dreaming. Or a partnership where professional and domestic responsibilities are higher than average, but are shouldered and celebrated by both of you.

Relationships where doing "work" (professional, spiritual, emotional) is prioritized in your lives and its importance is respected by both of you equally, is an extremely useful expression of the energy inherent to this placement, and a remedy against having it foisted upon you from external sources. Saturn is a planet that truly appreciates digging into something hard, something that will take time, elbow grease and perseverance to achieve, together. Any goal that you two choose consciously to undertake is far more rewarding than having something chosen for you. Decide to write a book together. Restore a house together. Caretake a family member. Build a business. Raise a family. It may feel burdensome at times, and exhausting. As the phrase goes: anything worth achieving is worth working hard for. At day's end, just make sure it is something you want to be doing.

If you, at some point in your life, undertake a partnership or domestic situation that feels especially restrictive, remember that it is always your decision to do so, and it is totally voluntary on your part. Even if you find yourself in a difficult situation no one else would desire but you willingly undertake, your decision to own your voice and authority within it changes everything. You become the hero with the superpowers instead of the old reliable doormat. Likewise, no commitment is so do-or-die that it cannot be revisited, reversed or altogether withdrawn from. Family guilt, loyalty, obligation to family, are likely sensitive subjects for you. You owe it to yourself to release any patterns of being guilted into doing things you don't want to do.

As a result of events of a past life, or this one, you may feel fearfully hesitant, or cautiously wary about whether domestic happiness is possible. You may feel a domestic partner or family could restrict or unduly burden you. Remember, the work for you is to not re-enact the difficulties you've already faced, and mastered, by silently placing yourself on the back burner due to necessity. The work is to honestly

108

face what you need to do to take care of yourself, without caving in to others' perceived incapacities, no matter how convincing or real they may be. You have more authority and leadership in your domestic realm than you probably think. Step up and own that.

A real path to fourth house Saturn happiness is a well-chosen partner who resembles the best of Saturn—who is responsible, has integrity, the patience to endure difficulty, maturity. In short, *one who is as capable as you.* They may be more mature than others. Good, they should be; maturity is a quality of character, not an age. You want an equal for a mate. They need to be able to take on that hard project you need to do, together. Be wary of partners who are needy, childlike or outright irresponsible since they will be an easy hook for you. Likewise, watch out for the perennial "stick in the mud"—a curmudgeonly, authoritarian partner. You don't want to marry a prohibitive patriarch, or your least favorite schoolteacher.

With Saturn here, home and family offer you chances to step into greater self-authority and integrity with yourself. There's no greater opportunity to live in integrity than by taking on a vow to love and respect one another, and when you can't, vowing to figure it out. Likewise, these same people can also show you where you need to take a hard line, and stand up for you. Sometimes love isn't enough.

Within a partnership, you may need to work on: not allowing obligations to own you, facing fears that a committed vow holds for you, owning an authoritative voice in your partnership, taking too much responsibility for others' limitations, bad habits or shortcomings…but do the above, and you achieve mastery. Always with Saturn, the authority you claim (or give away), in both partnership and with family, sets the tone for your experience. Claim your authority. No one can give that to you, but you!

There's No Place Like Om

Every fourth house planet needs privacy, but Saturn needs its privacy *respected.* Just as a house needs walls and doors to house its members, and no one questions that fact, you unquestioningly need privacy for yourself. Ideally, you have a room of your own—a place where your solitary hermit side has permission to do whatever you like.

With Saturn, it needn't be big, a little goes a long way. You might put a tiny house on your property, and use it as your art studio or office. Maybe you cannot afford an extra room, but you do have a special corner of the backyard garden that calls your name, and when your partner sees you in that part of the garden, they know it means you don't want to be disturbed—because you have authoritatively told them that, and they respect it, and you. Verbal boundaries can be as, if not more, powerfully effective than those of walls and doors.

Since Saturn appreciates old things, you may enjoy living in an old Victorian, or similarly old house. Or, because of your can-do, you might enjoy taking on a fixer-upper project that requires your dedication and time. In all areas of life, you devote care and attention with making sure things feel solid, reliable, safe and durable, and that applies to your home. You are deeply attuned to safety and security, so you don't want to take any shortcuts when it comes to doing what it takes to make your home feel safe, secure and structurally solid.

Saturn appreciates home-based comforts that allow you to be efficient and effective in life. Little things like having a bathtub, a washer-dryer in your own home, or a dishwasher are worth figuring out how to make happen. These practical little things add up to a big difference for you, helping you to feel you are deeply taking care of yourself. Also, because Saturn loves having all necessities addressed & covered, these resources free up your time for other important things, like roller skating, or having drinks with friends!

Your quiet kid could be: a hermit, old Soul, Benjamin Buttons, a medicine man/woman, a businessperson, wry comic or comedienne, the boss of "me!"

Your fourth house familiars: are old Souls, committed (show up/do when they say they will), mature, wise, have a dry wit, follow-through, integrity.

Your fourth house familiars are not: irresponsible, immature, curmudgeonly, repressive, lacking integrity, fearful of commitment.

Ancestral healing: release ancestral blockages around social correctness, duty, commitment, hardship and limitation. Someone in your lineage may've been overly conditioned by keeping pace with the status quo, lacked the developmental and practical resources to work through a loss/hardship, was long-suffering, depressive. Heal this for yourself: prioritize your happiness, release unfulfilling, time-serving obligations, choose to undertake responsibilities and agreements consciously, claim your authority and voice in partnership, respect your need for creative solitude.

Your hidden treasure: your persistent resourcefulness, your able willingness to tackle any mountain or difficulty no matter how high or impossible-seeming is your magic mojo. Don't underestimate this steadfast fearlessness you have, guided by your innate sense of integrity, always wanting to do the right thing— or your capacity to be a role model for others in all the above regards. Think about how a mountain climber gets to the top of the mountain: they don't fearfully, fretfully look down or up, wondering if they'll ever get where they want to be. Instead, they take it one step at a time, trusting their feet and hands to find the right, next place. *You really do know what you're doing.* Show this face of yourself to the world.

Uranus in the Fourth House, or Aquarius on the Cusp: The Quiet Individualist

Devon knew they loved him, but he also knew that his biological family was unlike him in almost every way possible. Devon was a spiritually sensitive Soul, interested in human dynamics, exploration and travel, while his family, to his mind, lacked curiosity about the world, other humans and their inner selves. When younger, he often felt excluded from the easy similarities and affection family members mirrored in one another, so much so that he had wondered whether he was adopted! When differences would pop up—in the way his parents didn't know how to engage or relate to Devon on his most important values, like his artistic self-expression, or grief around the passing of a close friend—Devon would feel, around family, deeply alienated and alone. As though he didn't truly belong.

If you were born with Uranus in the fourth house, you can probably relate. The fourth house is the house of belonging, with which oddball Uranus, at least at first glance, seems intrinsically at squares. With Uranus here, you did not fit in with your biological family. In reality, they were as different from you as you were from them. But for children, survival depends on fitting in, lest we risk rejection from the same group we need to protect, clothe and house us. If we express different viewpoints, color our hair purple or have divergent life goals, we hope that they will not turn us out to the wolves! At various points in history, for children, this has been a reality.

Socially, it has been dangerous to be an outlier, different from the norm. With Uranus in the fourth house, this precarious reality presents itself in your biological family—at least during childhood. Karmically, or in this lifetime, your unique individuality was squelched, unrecognized or unsupported by early family members.

The good news is, you've reached a place where, today, with your chosen family and committed partner, *in the very way you choose to live your life*—you simply must be yourself. This has less to do with rebelling against the norm (though it can look that way) or needing a lot of freedom with partners, and more to do with you giving yourself permission to choose a lifestyle which supports your authentic individuality—without caring how that looks to other people, or what they say they want or need from you.

That last phrase is the clincher for Uranus. There are certain things in life we each must do to remain in alignment with our True Self, and these may be very different from what the world, or loved ones, want from you. You feel this acutely at various points in your life. As such, your Soul wants to develop a lot more indifference to all the social codes of belonging, judgment, guilt and conditioning—basically the "shoulds" in life that limit you from self-actualizing, and instead to value the authentic aliveness of charting your own course.

In truth, the very things that seemed to be a liability in your family of origin—your different-ness, the way you never quite fit in—are your treasure. This gave you the necessary detachment to pursue a life governed only by one person's opinion—YOURS!

Restore and Renew

The world at large has an opinion about just about everything. From how you should eat, to what car you should drive, to what workout you should do. The advice will differ by sub-cultures and geography—for instance, what you should be driving in Marin, California (a luxury SUV) will be different from what you should be driving in Lincoln, Nebraska (a minivan). But at the end of the day, we are so shaped by the group-think of our environment that it's sometimes hard to separate what we truly want and like from what the people around us are telling us that we should want and like.

You are exceptionally sensitive to this kind of social pressure. It is imperative, throughout life, that you attempt to shake off ideas about what everyone else in your environment is telling you that you should want, their values, and discover your own. One of the best ways to do this is by exploring activities, interests outside of your local culture. If everyone is going to Mexico on vacation, try someplace else. If yoga is the craze, do you really love it? Do you wear the latest fashion trend in your community, or do you chart your own course? What cultural narrative or bandwagon do you jump on too easily, almost reflexively? In short, if "everyone else is doing it," be wary.

For instance, there is a collective fantasy inherent to romantic relationship and committed partnership, generally, in our culture: the white picket fence of home ownership, marrying and having children by a certain age, and someone of a particular background, sexual orientation or social status. Any of these may be Soul cages for you. Not all of us need the same things, but society will gladly sell us the story that we do. You are much happier when you are free of cultural constructs for your happiness. That's, in fact, how you find it.

At your core, you feel your most alive and free when you have broken away from arbitrary values that have no true place in your life. Even the ones that sound good. Careful, it can be very easy to align yourself with a battle, ideal or social cause, because other people are thinking it and it sounds like the right thing to do. This may take some wrestling with. After all, we each have considerable conditioning to un-do in life. As you age, especially as you pass your mid-life Uranus opposition (ages 40-44, approximately), you grow more honest with yourself and it becomes incrementally easier to recognize what is true for you. You discover delicious freedom, to do and be who you damn well please. And, you realize, this authenticity is not worth any price that belonging would ask of you.

Your Soul Mate(s) and Tribe

Chances are, your family of origin had the effect of making you feel like a stranger in your own home and family. Since we can easily be attracted to what's familiar, even if it's extremely uncomfortable, not fitting in, and general dis-resonance with loved ones who do not understand you is that uncomfortable old shoe, that "old familiar feeling" you learned to accommodate out of necessity long ago. Good news: you no longer have to!

You get to decide who you want in your family today. Embrace this freedom. The ability to choose our own partners and path in life, without fear of persecution, is a relatively recent freedom for many. What will your chosen family look like? Your natural tribe members will walk their own path, and respect your individuality because they are individuals themselves. They don't "should" you into decisions, goals or dreams that aren't yours. They don't discourage you from things they are afraid of or don't understand. They support your happiness and your heart's truth, whatever that looks like for you (not just when it is convenient for them). They are not threatened by differences between you, your growth trajectory, but are excited by it all. Differences will arise, but these are the spice of life!

Since on a Soul level you remember being in a family or intimate partnership that has stifled your authentic expression, you don't want to re-enact this early family conflict by marrying a partner who thinks you're "too weird," argues your preferences, choices, truths and is frankly a little afraid of the very things you need and want to express in life—your Soul's authentic truth.

Likewise, be open to change when the need for it arises. One's authentic truth is an ongoing process of self-discovery. We don't always want for ourselves today what we wanted yesterday. We are always awakening, changing, and that makes life surprising and yummy. Your ideal relationship accommodates your unique growth path, allowing you to change as your interests and enthusiasms do. Maybe one day you get turned on by astrology, then you take a class, and the next thing you know you are becoming a professional. Maybe a career aspiration requires you to make a dramatic move to another locale. Is your partner blown away and turned on by this new expression, or blown out? The best kind of partnership is one that can adapt to and accept all the different people you become in the course of a lifetime while loving the constant YOU all along.

There's No Place Like Om

There are no rules when it comes to how each of us needs to live. For one person, a house with two separate wings—one for each partner—is totally appropriate, yet for another person, that same design will feel inauthentic. There's no right or wrong. Both are equally true...and yet both cannot be simultaneously true in the same house. The key is finding the right match between you and another. The way to do that is to really know yourself.

Take, for instance, what level of space you need in your own home. Everyone requires different levels of space and privacy. Some are okay living like puppies, communally all piled on top of one another; others need more space than the average person. Again, it's all good, but when it comes to cohabitating with your fourth house familiars, define what you need. Get to know what's most important for you to feel safe, loved and free. Someone else's idea of domestic bliss may not be the same as yours. When you aren't on the same page about the way you want to live—from the division of labor and household chores, to caretaking family members, to saving for retirement—their version of domestic bliss can become your domestic trap.

However, and wherever, you decide you need to live (the sky is the limit for you), you need to feel like you can be yourself, at home and with family. One of the greatest adult pleasures of having a home to call all your own is that, yes, in this space, you can do your own thing. Need to let off some steam? Have a dance party. Naked! If you want to paint your staircase purple and write love poetry on it, go for it. Want a bedroom that allows you to sleep under the stars—why not? In your home and marriage, self-expression and egalitarian individuality should be encouraged for all members. There are no rules about what your home (or marriage) should look and feel like. And those who tell you there are, aren't people you want to live with!

Your quiet kid could be: a little individualist, a little genius, a Mensan, rebel, loner, outcast, quirky, different from all the others.

Your fourth house familiars are: authentic, exceptionally intelligent, different from the rest, quirky, individualistic, freedom-loving.

Your fourth house familiars are not: overly-dependent, autocratic, rebellious just to be contrary, threatened by change and different-ness.

Ancestral healing: release ancestral blockages around being different or being rejected for living outside the norms of social conventions. Someone in your lineage may've been a rebel, an outlaw, and was punished for being different from the rest of the family. This caused a degree of trauma. Since ancestral memories reverberate throughout time and space, work to release fears of rejection so you don't have to move through life attracting what you most fear. Consciously choose a family, home, homeland, where you don't have to hide any part of yourself to feel safe and loved. More deeply, don't look to others to make you feel you belong. You belong. Period.

Your hidden treasure: okay, you may have been judged, rejected, and left alone...but because you know what it's like to feel different, to not fit in, you are exceptionally accepting of differences. Others feel accepted around and by you. When you know you don't need to fit in to belong, you just being you is healing for the rest of us. What's in your treasure chest? A feather boa? An unlived dream? A truth? Open up your most authentic self by doing that "crazy" thing—be willing to stand in your truth without caring how others feel. You may shock loved ones, but they'll secretly admire you for it.

Neptune in the Fourth House, or Pisces on the Cusp: The Closeted Mystic

Zen had always been very sensitive. He knew when a friend or loved one was upset or hurt, sometimes he sensed when someone he loved was in trouble from far away, and he even occasionally had visionary nighttime dreams that would come true…yet very few people knew of his psychic sensitivity. By day, he was a lawyer who used logic and reason to address the world's injustices and social ills. He knew how to play hardball and was known as one of the strongest attorneys around. Only those very close to him knew that he had these intuitive gifts, which he sometimes used in ways other people could only guess at. On more than one occasion his professional calls were eerily spot on, for no other reason than he listened to his gut.

Zen's childhood fostered a need for retreat, as his home life often felt chaotic. His father was often absent for long stretches of time and Zen suspected he had a mental health and addiction problem that no one wanted to face. To soothe himself young Zen loved escaping into nature and playing fantasy games, alone, and as an adult he used long solitary walks in nature and plenty of time spent in meditation to recenter and counteract the stressors of urban living.

Like Zen, you have a softer, mystical side, a reflective and naturally inward-looking orientation which the external world may not readily see, and you may not openly share. This may be in reaction to this or prior lifetimes in which your imaginative, spiritual nature was diminished by family members, and/or your home life was chaotic and lacked cohesion—for instance, due to an absent or ill parent. Conversely, perhaps you spent time in a monastery, developing your spirituality. Spiritual, intuitive and psychic awareness may be in common vernacular now but this form of knowing has not been socially supported, historically. Yet it is inherent to who you are today. Your magical, romantic, mystical and even psychic side is felt.

Neptune and the fourth house overlap nicely in their shared aim of nurturing the life of the Soul and of the imaginative psyche through reflection, inwardness, beauty and spiritual explorations, but where Neptune appears we are also prone to distortions that arise from fantasy, projection, confusion, and the seeking of perfection where it may not exist. For you, finding the perfect home, partner and domestic life can remain an elusive source of yearning that, like a siren's call, takes you away from the present moment. The way through this is accepting that others are truly doing the best they know how, understanding that any idea you have of perfection is more malleable than you think (and you have power to influence) and discovering the freeing acceptance of embracing what is.

Restore and Renew

Nothing is more restorative for you than relaxing, or better yet living, next to a body of water. Not only does this balance your emotions, water helps you to ground. If you are not geographically near an ocean, lake or stream, even a fountain in your office will help you maintain equanimity. There's a reason why the gentle sound of trickling water, or the lapping waves of the ocean, play in the background of almost every hypnosis recording ever made—water is naturally calming, mesmerizing!

More than frequent vacations at the beach or near water, to stay centered, you need regular doses of healthy escapism. One of the drawbacks of being so sensitive is that you sponge up energy you may not realize you're absorbing. Media, the congestion of living in an urban environment, ongoing environmental stress and intensity of modern times…all generate energy. Like a cup being filled past its brim, you can become too full of external junk, which causes you to feel bad, so you naturally seek release of some sort. To feel good again, Neptune needs a certain quality and kind of release—*a genuine escape from it all*—but too often that falls into shadowy kind: too much time spent online, watching television or a few glasses of wine every night to "unwind." These quick fixes don't work in the long run.

What will give you the relaxing escape you crave? Here are some ideas: A front row seat in your home stereo system listening to your favorite musician, bird-watching over a cup of tea every morning, the regular reading of poetry, weekly gardening sessions, pottery lessons and star-gazing…as would a regular appointment quietly staring at the ceiling. All accomplish Neptune in the fourth house's Soul need for you to slow down, be present, steep in the stillness of this moment. Thus, any time you spend in "time outside time," that is, time spent without a goal in mind, without watching the clock, with, nothing to do, nowhere to go and no one to be, is infinitely restorative for you—you re-fill your cup with pure light energy and unconsciously absorb less junk from the world around you.

For Neptune, staying too busy and then filling one's downtime with unhealthy escapism is a good way to become moody and miserable. When we are overly focused on survival issues, paying the rent, external accomplishment and worldly works, our un-integrated Neptune can leave us feeling empty and wondering why we feel like a ghost in our own life, at least in our private one. Or why we feel we're drifting through life, rootless. Or why we don't live in a place we love. We may be accomplished in our career, and have every external base covered, but when we close our eyes at night, there's an aching and yearning for something…more. It can be hard to put our finger on with Neptune, but finding out what that is for you begins with actually heeding the more "irrational" calls of your heart and Soul. To get still enough to listen to your heart's guidance, stop distracting yourself. Stop putting simple presence off.

When you give yourself time to inwardly connect, you remember there is no separation. You feel this truth: we are all One. For you, the bottom line is the same as it is for everyone, though infinitely more pressing for you to resolve: who has time to prioritize mediation, music and activities that nourish the Soul but don't necessarily create external worldly value? No one. But what's the alternative? Rootlessness, a sense of disconnection, feeling out of your center. Your personal evolution, like much of humanity's, relies on this.

Your Soul Mate(s) and Tribe

Imagine coming home at the end of the day to a house mate who is plugged into the computer or television all evening, every evening. You ask about their day and get a few indiscernible responses. Distraction seems to be a permanent state for them; they have checked out. This is not ideal for you. In an alternate scenario, you come home to a partner who is enjoying the view of the ocean from your deck. As you share your day, and they theirs, you feel an alive connection between you. This has less to do with what you are actually saying to one another and more to do with the quality of energy, of presence. You feel them listening with your whole being; you listen with your whole being, though "listening" hardly describes it. Time ceases to exist. It is a quality of being nowhere else but here. *You are both one hundred percent right here.* This is palpable, and wonderful.

Your most intimate partners, Soul tribe and Soul family are those who innately understand what the above paragraph means. Not everyone has the capacity to be as Neptunian as you need. It's kind of like music appreciation—if you don't have the ears to hear it, you can be in the presence of an extremely gifted artist and have no idea that what you are listening to is the most angelic, amazing, and out-of-this-world music ever.

The thing about Neptune people is, *they know.* They know why you cry when you hear certain songs. They know why you need to stand under the light of stained-glass windows in that famous cathedral you visit together, quietly, and for as long as you need. They know why your ancestral stories are vitally important for you to understand. They know to trust your "I can't explain why I need to do this thing, but I just feel I do…" hunches. There are things you can never understand or explain to someone who doesn't "get it." A Neptune person simply, naturally, knows. *They know these things.*

Yet it would be a mistake to expect a fantasy Neptune ideal from your loved ones. That's a risk with Neptune: projecting your need for sensitivity and spiritual inwardness onto a spiritually-oriented, ever-present perfect partner who full body "listens" to your re-telling of your most recent past life regression on your ocean view deck. You may as well demand a bottle of French champagne, too! Jokes aside, the reality is that you hold the bigger piece of this quality of energy, both to your Soul tribe and intimate partnership. It is up to you to hold this energy. Don't expect another to do for you what you have not figured out already to do for you. Because like attracts like, and because we are all connected in ways we cannot fathom, the more connected you are to this part of yourself, so ALL become. As you embrace your spiritual side, you will draw it out from those you love.

That's a hopeful caveat for those of you in a partnership thinking, "Omg, my person is not Neptunian at all!" It's a bit of synchronicity at work for you here. You may not believe you are with the perfect Neptunian partner, but as you give yourself permission to follow your spiritual, non-linear yearnings—to attend that poetry workshop, study with the metaphysical teacher, have that session with the healer, massage therapist, or psychic you've been wanting to try—the more likely you are to be delightfully surprised by just how Neptunian they are. They magically become better "listeners" simply because you are becoming more present and in tune with yourself.

Likewise, it would be tragic for you to claim a Soul family that is dismissive toward the magic and wonder of the world—and of you.

There's No Place Like Om

Here's a thing I can say about your most desirable living situation, with nearly 100% accuracy. Your fantasy home would naturally feature the following: quiet, seclusion, privacy, a bit of romance (a little cottage) and/or glamour (an architect's dreamhouse), and be near or on water. Those with Neptune in the fourth house are drawn toward living on water, and in my experience that yearning only gets stronger over time. Many of my fourth house Neptune clients have found themselves heading into retirement years and toward the sea, the urge to be near water becoming almost unbearably hypnotic.

Whenever possible, choose calming, restorative, meditative environments and décor. You might enjoy a lot of white and neutral natural colors in your home, or softer pastels, since relaxed colors will soothe your nervous system. Reflective metals like gold and silver bring in light and softness. Fountains, gardens, and tucked away places for you to retreat to are also helpful. Nurture your softer, more subtle, mystical side through how you choose to live at home.

You are sensitive—to your environment, to energies of others and to how you spend your free time. Honor this. A sacred space will always nurture you. Treat your home as you would a sacred space. A sacred space might feature candles, incense, spiritual figures, have soft music. It might have the energetic air of a centuries old church having witnessed millions of people in worship, or of a timeless and meticulously maintained garden. Sacred space feels like home to you.

Finally, where Neptune is, a degree of fantasy follows. You may have a fantasy that there is a perfect home or living situation waiting for you, somewhere, if only you can find it. The perfect home (or marriage) can take on a mythical, aspirational, quality. But there's a catch-22: this state of yearning for something else will always take you out of the present moment, which in turn creates dissatisfaction. If this is you, call off the search for otherworldly perfection! Stop looking for fulfillment outside of yourself, because that won't ever happen. Instead, focus on what offers you bliss, right now. Be present. For any true need, trust Divine Timing will take care of it.

Spiritual and wellness practices are forms of exquisite self-care, and non-negotiable for you. As are tribe members who support your need for the domestic realm to be Neptunian: peaceful, sacred, reflective. Your awareness of energy and aesthetics transcends any trendy lifestyle choice but is a deeply vitalizing way to share your Soul's gifts. Your Soul is worth nurturing, allowing, supporting. When you allow the sacred to shine through you, everyone benefits.

Your quiet kid could be: a little mystic, a daydreamer, an otherworldly creature, a true believer, poet, secret romantic, extravagant fantasizer.

Your fourth house familiars are: spiritual, soulful, accepting, nurturing, they "know" things that you don't have to explain.

Your fourth house familiars are not: materialistic, rigid, insensitive, closed-minded, judgmental, dismissive of magic, spirituality and mystery.

Ancestral healing: release ancestral blockages around spirituality, magic and sensitivity. Someone in your family lineage may've mysteriously disappeared or been absent—because of health issues, or they chose to check out or escape due to overwhelm, sensitivity saturation. Heal this by honoring your need for a higher than average amount of time spent in spiritual consciousness. Release self-judgment, work on self-acceptance. Don't distract yourself from yourself to the point that you feel bereft and want to escape, too. Allow yourself to spend time outside of time. Meditate. Prioritize downtime, imagination and artistic and spiritual self-expression.

Your hidden treasure: you are a closeted mystic; bring him or her out of the closet occasionally. Your innate understanding of the interconnectivity of life, its inherent beauty, means you deeply value exploring what it means to be a spiritual being in a human body. Whether you attribute your ease with the spiritual realm to your intuitive perception, your boundless compassion, or having logged many hours in a monastery in a past life, recognize this in yourself. It doesn't really matter how you "know," but that *you know you do know!* Integrate your Neptune more deeply into your consciousness and those who naturally "get it" and "know" get to see this deeper you.

Pluto in the Fourth House, or Scorpio on the Cusp: The Perceptive Detective

Like a moth to a flame, Antoinette was attracted to the dark side of life. She loved horror movies, especially the B-list ones with campy sex scenes. Equally, she loved reading psychological dramas and mystery novels; her favorite ones usually involved a detective, an astrologer, a witch, a romance or better yet—all of the above!

Those who knew Antoinette well could always count on her to pull no punches, and whether it was advice, or commentary on the latest political scandal, she tended to pierce right into the juicy, real and often taboo heart of things, which served her well as a writer. With those she loved, she didn't believe in the "if you have nothing nice to say, don't say it at all" policy. Not that she wasn't nice; she was just more sensitive than most to what begs to be acknowledged, but is hidden due to embarrassment, shame or fear. She wanted to know and name truth, and she could smell untruth a mile away.

Of course, there was a reason for this uncanny skill. In Antoinette's early childhood, much went unsaid. Hard truths were pushed under the dinner table like unwanted lima beans. It was bad. Her parent's dysfunctional relationship was evident to Antoinette, as was domestic abuse she occasionally accidentally walked in on more than several times in her childhood. Honesty was traded for holding everything together. Her parents just weren't able to squarely face their problems. As a result, Antoinette felt unsafe and conflicted: on one hand she loved them, but on the other she didn't trust them to protect or look out for her best interests. Now, as an adult, she astutely noticed she was suspect about the possibility of ever having domestic bliss herself, jaded even. With reason, she thought. Her first marriage was a disaster—they fought all the time and it got verbally abusive in the end. She hadn't quite healed from that.

Where Pluto is, we have experienced deep wounding. We all have Pluto in our chart, so none of us escape this. With Pluto in the fourth house, you have a wound revolving around family and clan bonds. Whether through omission of damaging truths, willful repression, neglect, abuse, or any other number of dysfunctions, with Pluto in the fourth, chances are as a child you were hurt by the very people who are supposed to love and protect you. This likely left some marks on you, like a subtle wariness about whether domestic happiness is possible for you, and a need to ferret out the truth.

A wounded fourth house Pluto can erect a fortress so solid that nobody will be able to find the front door. Yet depth of understanding and wholeness is only acquired by facing the darker realities of life, not avoiding them or running away from pain. To this end, you have remarkable gifts of insight—an ability to deeply see into human behavior, your own and others, to sense what's been hidden or buried, and you can address what most people don't want to talk about with great skill and compassion. This truly insightful perceptiveness makes you a good witch of the best kind!

Restore and Renew

I once had a client, with Pluto in the fourth house, who said, "I had a great childhood, no complaints at all. Pretty vanilla, boring, actually!" I was naturally suspect. Pluto is a planet with a story far longer than one sentence or page. Where we find Pluto in the chart, we also find core wounding. With Pluto here, family showed you your first experience of love, and they showed the darker side of that, too.

Today, your Soul needs to face difficult emotional, physical or psychological wounds from your family of origin in order to not re-create them with your new family. Your true Soul tribe can handle it. They understand the importance of psychological work. They know that we all have baggage comprised of old hurts, misunderstanding, because they have identified and worked on theirs, too.

There are landmines to watch out for, though. Sometimes, Pluto, who has a penchant for remaining in control and not ever getting hurt *like that* again, gives rise to defense mechanisms. Perhaps there are whole areas of our inner self that we choose not to explore or engage because that would mean we'd have to feel what we don't want to feel, where we were once made to feel powerless, ashamed, abandoned, judged, less-than. Yet when we turn our back on our shadows we also turn away from our light. We may wonder why we can't sustain a partnership, or why we feel negative and tired all the time. It takes enormous energy to keep areas of our essence buried and unconscious. Likewise, it takes persistence, patience, time, therapy of some form and endless honest, investigative conversations with oneself to heal. Either way you slice it, this is not easy stuff! However, this is the path to feeling empowered and whole.

You are equipped for it. You have a deep reservoir of hidden psychic strength—your capacity for renewal and transformation is certain. You not only can survive anything, you can, like a starfish, grow a new limb should you need one. Your Soul is eternally whole. There is no past that is so damnable you can't recover from it. Nothing true can ever be taken away from us; it may temporarily disappear, but will be given back in time. If your innocence or trust were violated, recover the power that was taken from you. Your most direct method is to journey back to that point in time when you felt traumatized, helpless and powerless, and heal where you were fractured. Once you've done this you can offer it to other people, or through a larger calling. Become a truth-teller, healer or shaman, someone who can capably point out what is hard to name or see with the naked eye. Advocate for victims of violence or oppression. Speak to what is taboo in culture; there can never be enough truth tellers.

But first, heal yourself. You restore yourself through going into the depths of your truthful experience. Turn your psychic perceptiveness gently toward your feeling life. Become a detective in your own emotional life. Journal. Create art. Express the full range of your emotional experience, including grief, traumas, abuses and the hard to voice truths, from a place of compassionate healing and unyielding self-acceptance. If you don't, stormy emotions can wreak havoc on your life happiness, cause you to say things you wouldn't normally say to someone you love, or to emotionally shut down from a place of wounding. Bottom line: either choose to become the person who has healed their past, and so compassionately speaks the truth of their experience, or you will be the person who throws their unprocessed hurt and pain onto other people. There is a difference.

Your Soul Mate(s) and Tribe

We don't need to be privy to all of our loved one's innermost thoughts. As a Scorpio friend once said to his partner when she claimed he didn't share enough with her, "Trust me, you don't want to know what I'm thinking!" It isn't always helpful to talk about it. Yet sometimes it is. To respect one another's privacy is essential, but when a real conversation doesn't happen at a critical moment, that is called avoidance, which can lead to big problems down the road.

Especially if there's a real issue to address. Let avoidance go on long enough and darker thoughts will consume you. You love them but you feel yourself growing resentful. You snap more often. You become short-tempered; you have more patience with a five-year-old. That's the direction avoidance often takes. It's also how you know you are close to identifying any core hurts you have yet to heal.

Relationships are a hotbed for projection and blame. Maybe, you think, with issues like *that*, your loved ones are easy to blame! While that may be true…it can only ever be half the truth. Few people know how to skillfully untangle their own stuff from their partners, but you were born to do this kind of psychic surgery on yourself.

Imagine, in this spirit, you take a deep and honest look at your own motives and behavior. Lately, you feel unappreciated by your partner, and you are angry about it. They are not living up to what you want from them in the relationship, which you are using against them *just as your mother did with your father*. Now you are getting somewhere. The conflict is no longer about what they are doing to you, which rarely shifts anything, but about how to come back into your own energy body and volition. You have the power to make yourself happy or unhappy, not your partner. When you own this, everything shifts.

With Pluto here, your commitment to self-honesty is crucial to feeling empowered to co-create, and to truly have, anything you want in life. This includes looking at wounded perceptions that shape your less attractive responses to life, and to those dearest to you. Your Soul's mates need this of you, too. Your tribe members are Plutonian; you are Plutonian. Even if hearing it initially makes you angry or uncomfortable to hear, they will bring up *the thing you don't want to deal with*. Perhaps it is that one thing you'd rather do just about anything else than to directly face! You likely bring that kind of stuff up for them, too. This the type of truth telling work your mates are here to help you walk through. And at day's end, you are grateful to work it out with them, someone you deeply love, rather than anyone else.

We are all humans here. None of us can truly see our own shadow; we all have baggage and backsides we cannot see. Your intimate partners help you honestly see the sides of yourself you have a hard time seeing alone, as you help them see theirs. With forgiveness, humility and kindness, you can achieve the deepest, most loving and loyal experience of intimacy. Just remember, though, your Soul tribe and partner(s) are not your therapist, nor are you theirs. There's no quicker way to kill love than having an armchair psychologist for a mate—someone who puts their self in a superior position of "knowing exactly what your problem is" while they remain somehow spotless and eerily perfect. That's how resentment grows, not love.

There's No Place Like Om

Privacy at home is paramount for you. You might enjoy the anonymity of being in the heart of a busy urban center, yet insularly buried in an apartment of a larger condominium complex. Or perhaps you live in the middle of nowhere with a quiet starry sky all to yourself. Pluto likes having the option of hiddenness, concealment, of going invisible. Privacy, for you, offers a psychological sense of protection, an ability to retreat from the world, along with the feeling of being in control of your space, of feeling safe.

Your Soul's mates will respect your need for privacy, to tool around doing inner work, play with tarot cards, or creatively focus. They will respect the energetic and psychic boundaries that you need because they have them, too. They know that much more happens in a day, in our psyches, than we can ever possibly hope to understand, and we all need time and space to just be and process things.

The home is the abode of the Soul. Don't underestimate the importance of having a home you truly love and care for. Just as you wouldn't take a marriage partner for granted, investing time and energy in your domestic sphere makes a huge difference in how you feel internally. You may minimize the importance of home because it hurts too much to admit how disempowered you feel, or how disempowered you have felt in the past, with family and home. Neglecting your living space is one possible manifestation of this. Equally possible, you may feel very attached to your particular abode – as though your house were a body part, or beloved family member.

Feeling loved, and that you have presence and voice in your domestic space, is paramount to accessing deeper feelings of power and security—as is not neglecting what is going on underneath the surface of things. Oddly, when issues go unaddressed too long in your relationship, and within your innermost self, you may find the weirdest of *wyrd* (in the old sense of the word, meaning fate or destiny) occurring at home. You may discover mold, leaks, waste issues, termites, pests that hide…all symbolic reminders that what's invisible must now be brought to light, or it can cause damage. One client reported discovering a second, hidden, sewage system in her backyard shortly after being diagnosed with breast cancer. As a preventative, you might consistently ask yourself, "What is it I've been willfully hiding from myself? What need am I avoiding?"

No need to get spooky, though. Your Soul is always in charge of your experience. You've looked at your own skeletons. Your domestic haven includes: self-help books, friends who double as therapists, and partners who engage hard truths with equal parts fearlessness and humanity. As you aim for no skeletons in your closet, you discover that there are many companions who suit your taste perfectly.

Your quiet kid could be: a little sorcerer, psychologist, little detective, magic-lover, keeper of secrets, master of disguise, poker face.

Your fourth house familiars: are psychologically honest, compassionate, intensely feeling, deep, strong, have an innate understanding of humanity.

Your fourth house familiars are not: unwilling to look at their psyche, avoidant, disrespectful of your boundaries, bitter, nasty, mean-spirited.

Ancestral healing: release ancestral blockages around the honest expression of shadow material and wounding. Someone in your lineage may've concealed the dark truth of a situation—out of shame, guilt or fear of abandonment. This came at a great cost to the family. Heal this by addressing what they could not, in yourself. Understand how holding any taboo material has shaped you, and whether it has distorted or colored your perception of what's possible for you in life. Be a detective. Use your investigative powers to unlock what's been hidden inside you. Allow the light of consciousness in.

Your hidden treasure: your zeal for getting to the bottom of things keeps you intrigued your entire life. Think about how, as a child, you loved discovering hidden passageways, dissecting frogs, or breaking open a Magic 8 ball just to see how it worked. This innate love for all things that fascinate you infinitely serves you. To your detective skills, add copious compassion. From exposing the nuances of human behavior, why we do and feel what we do, to figuring out how to save the planet and sharing what you learn, your life choices can be that impactful. You have truth-tellers magic, so don't forget to open up, share your love for truth. The world needs it from you!

The South Node in the Fourth House:
The Family Man/Woman

The south node is not a planet in western astrology, it is a point, so it doesn't describe what you need from your new clan today. However, it does suggest that family of origin work, before you choose a new family, is a really good idea for you.

While your early home life held both positive and negative experiences, this placement indicates that some of the behaviors, conditioning and attitudes that accompanied being part of a family may be holding you back from expressing who you are today. For instance, deferring to others' needs, gaining consensus from other family members before making a personal choice, devoting oneself to the care and security of one's tribe can all be natural and positive motivations in a family. Yet with south node in the fourth house, these all carry a warning: it's easy for you to be absorbed by your family, and forget to bring your talents and gifts to the market. It's easy for your role in, and obligations toward, family to obscure you.

In the karmic past, you had strong ties to your family; your family or marriage may have defined you. Perhaps you earned a PhD in homemaking or caregiving, or your brood depended on you for their survival and protection. Now the time has come for you to offer your talents and skills to the world at large by pursuing a professional calling. The spiritual insight and gifts you've earned within the family need to publicly come out. You can still have a successful marriage or family experience, but you also have a high chance of re-creating conditions in this area that limit you. Look to your family of origin to investigate the sharp hooks and apron strings family holds over you, and learn how to avoid them (to learn more about what those are, be sure to read for the zodiacal sign of your south node).

133

Ancestral healing: releasing ancestral blockages around family and tribe itself. Someone in your lineage may've been too absorbed by family dynamics at a cost to their creative contribution. Heal this by resisting a strong pull to "settle down" right away, with all that implies (marriage, children, home ownership, etc.). Be open to finding a larger mission/calling. Be open to defining yourself as separate from the family unit.

The North Node in the Fourth House:
The Soul Mate

The north node is not a planet in western astrology, it is a point, and suggests an area in which you are least acquainted with and requires integration into your life. In the recent karmic past, you have spent plenty of time in the public eye developing yourself professionally. You were well-known by others as being someone of status or importance in the community, but this responsibility to reputation and community didn't give you the down time, or the privacy, to sink into your Soul.

The chief complaint any public person makes is lack of a private life. Whether you were famous or not, your focus on a public life has created an extreme imbalance in your home and private life. The time has come for you to undertake the unfamiliar process of drawing psychologically inward, nesting and rooting. This could start with becoming attached to a piece of land or a house you love. Setting up house with someone you love might be a challenging (but rewarding) adventure. Even if the thought of being domestic and settling into comfortable habits and patterns with another sounds like walking on the Moon to you, rest assured it is one of the most profound forms of intimacy that you will experience. You don't need to turn into a hermit or a homebody (though, for you, it's a good idea to try it!), but place importance on your interior, psychological and spiritual life.

Find the place and people with whom you can be your most un-self-conscious and comfortable. Prioritize the tenderness, love, loyalty and easy familiarity that accompanies being with loved ones with whom we call our familiars. Take the time to explore your inner world, to discover what gifts lay within your psyche, gifts that only quiet solitude can unlock. All of the above offer great opportunity for

135

your spiritual growth. For more about the specific type of energy required for a supportive home and domestic partnership for you, be sure to read the zodiac sign of your north node.

Ancestral healing: releasing ancestral blockages around being too caught up in a mission at the cost of the inner life and self. Someone in your lineage may've valued worldly action over introspection, achievement over the importance of a fulfilling home life. Heal this by making all fourth house matters (rooting, nesting, solitude, quiet, etc.) your guiding star.

Section 4: Your Roots Are Showing

"I've seen it before, and I'll see it again, it's all just a little bit of history repeating." - Propellerheads

One of my consistently favorite things to do with ongoing clients is to look at the charts of family members and notice the patterns. Themes always readily emerge, yielding many ooh, and a-ha moments. Ah, Libra and Pisces are consistently sprinkled throughout; that explains the family habit of co-dependency! Often, chart aspects repeat. Or sign and planet combinations. You can slice it dozens of different ways and see family patterns emerge.

I'm a Cancer Sun and South Node. I have always deeply felt the way energies of family shaped my self-perception. The charts of our family members offer more than a 3D glimpse into energies beyond time and space. They potentially link our everyday disappointments and dreams, struggles and blockages to that of our larger family. What's more, science is now validating this.

Science supports this link between our ancestral experiences and our DNA. Epigenetics is the field of science that studies the influence of our environment on gene expression. One epigenetics study found that mice who underwent traumatic stress early in life passed on that trauma marker to their children and grandchildren through their sperm, resulting in more anxious offspring (mice DNA are 97% similar to humans).

In human genome studies, we have already seen how heritable diseases are affected by environmental factors such as diet, exercise or toxicity, but this discovery about trauma that potentially links our current day *emotional health* to the experiences of our father or grandfather (this study was limited to male carriers of a chromosome) opens the door for considering other possibilities…and questions. Just how much are we affected by our ancestors' experiences? Is it possible that how they experienced their lives—the problems they faced and the subsequent limiting beliefs they formed around them—are unconsciously affecting us today, through our very genes?

The possibilities are mind-boggling. Yet if our genetic expression can be altered, we can change our own genome by reducing stress, healing trauma, altering our perceptions and beliefs, thus creating a trans-generational healing effect. In other words, we don't have to send dad's fear of failure down the family line into future offspring. We can stop the line right here!

This is an exciting discovery for science. Even if most of us who study astrology already suspected this was true, scientific validation can embolden us to entertain broader perspectives on our "issues." Sometimes in life we experience issues that plague us, the origins of which we cannot easily identify. Consider this: If something feels intensely personal, and yet not personal at all, or if it feels so much bigger than you…it may be connected to your ancestors.

Energy Work in the Fourth House

"The work of the eyes is done. Go now and do the heart-work on the images imprisoned within you." - Rainer Maria Rilke

One of the oldest definitions of the fourth house includes "ancestral inheritances"—items of other family members, bequeathed to us at their death. Inheritance is not always material. While some of us might inherit mom's pearls, or grandma's tea set, others of us inherit persistent relationship disappointment or a sense of shame we cannot explain. Because it feels so personal and yet so hard to put our finger on, we might even feel persecuted by what we experience here.

I've gone through periods of feeling ancestral energies surfacing energetically, as physical and emotional symptoms which I couldn't link to anything in my environment or being. It can be frustrating. I've walked around for weeks feeling asthmatic, unable to breathe properly, while knowing this symptom was connected to my paternal ancestral line. I've felt the rage of my female lineage, as apparitions of sudden, ice cold teeth-chattering chills of energy sweeping through my body. I've lifelong and diligently worked on myself to clear karmic relationship habits connected to family conditioning and ancestral energies. I've also dialogued with my lineage and received relief and recognition from the other side. I've felt deeply loved, supported and connected by my ancestors after their death.

There are many ways to work with the energies of your ancestors, some of which I will share with you in the following chapters. Working with them doesn't require a regressionist or medium. In fact, the simplest methods are often the best for accessing their energies. I have a client who now spends most of her time connecting with her ancestors as a family storyteller and genealogist. She was moved to work with them regularly, so started an online site, a family tree replete with their photos and life events, which she researches. Interestingly, she has made connections to patterns that present-day relatives appear to be re-experiencing today in their lives.

She's had energetic, sensory visitations, too. While working with a particular ancestor, she will often feel their energies emerge in her life. This is far from spooky for her; it is only ever sweet and healing. By telling their stories, she feels she is bringing them healing and acknowledgement. She's even made overseas visits to former ancestral residences in England and Ireland. Illuminating ancestral lives allows her to express her fourth house Sun in Sagittarius.

What are the benefits of giving time and attention to working with your fourth house in this way? Fourth house planets can indeed illuminate the family curse should we have one…but every curse contains its cure. The story behind your persistent blockage? It may also be *their* story. Through exploring, we can see patterns emerge, which, once conscious, no longer unconsciously plague us. With more awareness and freedom, we can choose more aligned Soul mates and have a more soulful experience of family. We can feel more connected to Oneness and our spiritual kinship to one and all.

If this idea appeals to you at all, it's no coincidence. Your ancestors are likely, eagerly, waiting for your recognition. With a little investigation, you may discover a connection to ancestors whose stories eerily mirror your particular dilemma, stories that by uncovering, acknowledging and re-telling, frees you. Mystical treasures—like feeling connected to spiritual realms beyond time and space—arrives through investigating our fourth house, too. Ask your ancestors; they may be more than happy to help

In that spirit, the following client experiences offer imaginative and easy ways of clearing fourth house energies.

Venus Therapy

At times, we all get stuck and need relationship help. Imagine your Venus has been sitting in a tucked away corner of unprocessed heartbreaks, disappointments and limiting beliefs piling up through the years. Wouldn't it be helpful to sort through it now and again?

Devi had read my book *A Love Alchemist's Notebook* and decided she wanted to do some Venus work with me. In her early thirties, she had recently filed for divorce from a two-year marriage. Before we began working together, she shared intimate details of her marriage.

Devi said, "I was the financial provider for the relationship, which caused problems in how he felt about himself. When we married, I wanted to give him the opportunity to focus on his art. Eventually, I felt I was becoming an empty shell—giving and not receiving back even when I asked for it. We had a long-distance relationship for part of the marriage. The final straw happened when we hadn't seen each other in a month and a half. We had yet to celebrate any anniversary or birthday together. When I had to postpone a visit, all he expressed was irritation because he needed my help doing his company's taxes."

Devi has Venus in Capricorn in the fourth house. Transiting Pluto would soon conjunct her Venus. Fourth house Pluto transits ask us to be excruciatingly honest with ourselves, especially related to home and family. Pluto asks us to closely attend to core wounds and misperceptions, family myths and sometimes family secrets.

We explored the many archetypal faces of Venus in Capricorn, including the "provider," the "responsible adult" and the "successful achiever." Devi identified with these images, and the idea that by being a successful little achiever, as a child, she could become the glue that held her parents' marriage together. "My parents weren't always happy together, but the one thing that united them was my accomplishments. I pushed myself hard in school. I became a national merit scholar and got my PhD, all things they could identify with. That gave them something to bond over."

We all adopt strategies to survive our childhood. Like a good little Libra Rising child, Devi had fallen into the trap of making everyone else happy at eventual cost to herself. Love from another is wonderful, but to a Venusian child, love is a survival strategy. Earning another's affection through being pleasing and cooperative can be a compulsive way of ensuring that "If you're okay then I am." Hard-working and accomplished, gaining scholastic recognition and awards, she had kept a semblance of peace in her parent's marriage.

However, dysfunctional childhood strategies cannot successfully translate into happy intimacy in adulthood. She was still being the good girl in her marriage, agreeing to take care of her partner's needs through the spoils of her achievements, but now it had backfired. She gave all her material, emotional, mental resources to him, worked all the time to provide, only to become an empty shell. She wanted a partnership with intimacy, sharing and reciprocity, not a business partnership. To make matters worse, her husband soon became jealous of her success, the same success that allowed him to move through the world with more ease. She had married a partner who actually resented her for her success—the ultimate betrayal because she was just doing exactly what she was "supposed to"!

By the time the marriage ended, she realized she had lost touch with Venus. Like most of us, she didn't know how to do anything differently than what she was doing. Devi's success had been over-valued for so long—by her parents, herself and to a degree, by her mate—that her Venus expression had become lopsided. Devi had already intuited this was a Venus problem. She said:

"I have Venus envy in that I'm not comfortable expressing or even being in the sensual, playful, sexual, and beautiful parts of myself. I tend to think of myself as a walking brain, unable both to connect to or express my emotions and to connect to the feeling and reality that I am a sensual and sexual and fun being. For years, my life has been about work, study and taking care of my partner to the extent that I feel like I lost myself and my joy. I want to reclaim those."

I asked Devi: *Who would you be without being "successful"?* It was a scary thought because it meant questioning the identity she'd maintained for so long. Yet answers poured out. About what and who she truly valued and loved in her life…about the aesthetic and creative side of herself she craved a more intimate connection with…about her desire for a mate to whom she could show her vulnerability, tenderness, and even be needy at times. She said, "I don't want to have to always hold it together, to be the strong, successful one all the time." The tight corset strictures of Venus loosened, giving her breathing room to explore and name what she'd been missing.

She also had another layer to push through, beliefs formed and passed down to her through her female line. Devi told me she didn't *believe* that love was possible for her. She said, "I have a pessimistic outlook about romantic relationship. With the writing prompt, 'Who would I be without my accomplishments?' came deep fear and a

142

sense that I was unlovable or not destined to be in a happy relationship. As I wrote, I felt this is something I have to work through but that it's also something that has been passed down by the women in my family, an ancestral burden that isn't mine, isn't my destiny."

Planets in any of the water houses (4, 8, 12) hold mysterious spiritual inheritances from our lineage. But this is a mixed blessing, because while there are clear gifts to eventually claim as our own, the shadow expression of that planet can obscure them. For instance, with Venus here, we have a lineage of artistic ability, gifts for making our home lovely and loved ones comfortable. First, though, we have to free our self from the family curse, so that we can turn it into a gift.

Devi's parents had divorced when she was seven years old. Neither remarried. Her mother had several relationships, ones where love "got away" through death or non-reciprocation. Her mother's mother, Devi's maternal grandmother, married her husband for wealth, staying unhappily together for fifty years. "She once mentioned to me that she wished granddad would die first so she could have time to herself." No such luck; granddad stuck around.

Devi's paternal grandmother was a gifted cellist who had won a scholarship to Julliard at age 18. She turned it down to get married. When the kids were grown, her grandmother plucked up the courage to leave the unhappy marriage and finally pursue the cello career she once abandoned, full time. She stayed single for the rest of her life.

If these three stories weren't enough to bring on goose bumps, the most dramatic of all was the story of her great-great-great-grandmother, adopted into a wealthy Jewish family in France. She fell in love with the eldest son, and together they had several children. A generous man, he constantly gave money away. When his generosity left the family impoverished, he went on a journey to find work. He felt he had failed them, so would earn the money back and redeem himself. He never returned, and her great-great-great-grandmother was heartbroken. The story goes that she became blind from crying.

Devi said, "I don't know if it's mine to break, but it seems as if this story of heartache repeats in women of every generation in my family." Our family histories often do read like a mystery novel. If we sleuth around enough, we may discover that our personal story contains many other stories, stories that can shed light on why we struggle with persistent invisible patterns. As astrologer and regression therapist Patricia Walsh has said, "You are not an island, and you stand at the end of a very long lineage that still lives within and around you through the spirits of your ancestors."

In her fabulous book, *The Astrology of Family Dynamics*, Erin Sullivan writes that in the fourth house, "We may run up against some mysterious blockage which we cannot explain…a haunting or deep sadness which may not be completely accounted for in the psychology of the immediate family." We might encounter this through a persistent belief that love is not for us, feelings of frustration, futility or a pessimistic outlook—as Devi had.

No matter how grim it looks, it can be comforting to know that when we acknowledge and honor our ancestors' stories, we can heal, too. Last we spoke, Devi's divorce was being finalized and she was working on an ancestral altar. Devi will transform her relationship with Venus. After all, *Devi* is the Sanskrit word for Goddess.

.

Exercise: Excavating Your Fourth House Planet

Devi had learned to earn love and approval from her parents by being successful at everything she did, at great cost to herself. Painfully, she discovered this by marrying a man who exposed her wounded way of being.

-Did you develop a way of surviving your childhood, behaviors that you are still using in your adult life that are unfulfilling and you no longer need?

144

-Look for any beliefs you have about what's possible (or not) for you, in life. Look for all-or-nothing statements, which usually have childhood origins. Statements like: "I'll never…" "I can't…" "It's always going to be this way…"

-Might these beliefs have been handed down through your ancestors? You can investigate the idea that your beliefs were formed as a result of a family or ancestral inheritance using techniques in the following chapters.

-Once you identify these beliefs, choose a way to clear or release them. You might build an altar, light a candle, or journal and then burn your words. You can comfortably sit or lay down, and envision your belief slipping away as easily as one releasing a balloon, or swiping right on a device. Whatever creative method you are drawn to try, be sure to fully feel any feelings and energies that arise; this is the most important step for clearing energies.

-Finally, replace this old belief with one that is true for you. How will you know if a belief is untrue? A false belief always feels emotionally uncomfortable. A true belief will feel peaceful. It will engage feelings of love, recognition and compassion toward yourself. Nothing true will ever feel bad, or cause you to feel bad about yourself.

Parent or Partner?

A therapist once told me that if two adult children of alcoholics are invited to a party that have no other alcoholics in attendance, these two people will find one another, guaranteed. While that theory may or may not actually prove true, like seeks like. Just as water can only reach its own level, those who are familiar or "like family" will hone in on each other like homing pigeons. It's as if our unconscious whispers: *Oh, you don't have a healthy relationship to your emotions? Neither do I. Let's get hitched!*

We often perceive instant comfort with another to be a really good thing. Consider this: familiarity and comfort with another can be a set up drawing us back into old childhood patterns. We feel a zip, zing, pizazz of chemistry…we feel as though we've known one another for years. And then the dysfunction ensues. The insecurities we have around them strongly resemble the way we felt when our mother criticized us. Or we realize we are dating our father's narcissism.

I'm not diminishing the value of feeling comfortable with our life mates; we need comfort with them to want to build a life together. However, in the last section, I suggested what's comfortable can be *uncomfortably familiar*. For instance, it's spooky how often people who have been abused as children later partner with abusers.

If we unconsciously attempt to recreate childhood patterns through our partners, what can we do? Obviously, it helps to get clear on what happened in our family of origin. For instance, do you really know why mom was so resentful, and dad so absent and withdrawn? Was there a point where fortunes or tides turned for your family? Did something traumatic happen? Was this ever addressed and healed, or did it leave a fault line in your foundation? If we grew up in a household where money was an attachment, either its lack or abundance generated lots of energy and focus, we need to do some therapy or inner work around that, otherwise we might re-create that same dynamic in our marriage. As the saying goes, inner work works.

I had a client whose family lost a fortune when she was very young. Almost overnight she went from being able to take horse riding lessons at the stables whenever she liked to having to save her pennies. The main issue in her marriage today? Not having enough money for the pleasures in life. She was consistently frustrated by not having a bigger house and income for travel. It was as if she was still trying to resolve that early childhood experience.

Understanding our roots, who we come from, their lifelong dreams and most bitter disappointments, what went unacknowledged, unsaid, left in the shadows, is preventative medicine. A form of immunity, it prevents us from experiencing the same in our chosen family.

Saturn Therapy

Judith had Saturn in Capricorn in her fourth house. When she first came to see me, her main complaint was that she was stuck in an unfulfilling marriage, to the point that she was already living in their city apartment. She was trying to figure out what went wrong. Of course, she still loved him, but she had been miserable for so long and she craved companionship. How had their relationship become so untenable?

When they first met, there was an instant kinship. Jim, a Capricorn Sun sign born, had an easy reliability, loyalty and steadfastness that appealed to Judith. He was a reliable presence in her topsy-turvy, sometimes chaotic world. To her, his strong sense of devotion and fidelity was proof he could be the rock she wanted in her life.

They married, acquired a farm and piece of land together. Jim was a great farmhand and he loved working outdoors. Judith had enjoyed city and country life, but country life began bringing her down. Judith craved excitement and stimulation. Jim didn't need intellectual engagement the way she did. Over time, the very things she was attracted to in him began to bug her. Judith was a free and passionate spirit with a tendency to push outside her comfort zone. That simply wasn't Jim. If she wanted a spontaneous romantic getaway, he would find ways of staying home, then she'd feel sabotaged. If she wanted to talk about some exciting new spiritual practice or philosophy she was exploring, he was unresponsive, dismissive or critical.

Sexually, they were at opposite ends of the spectrum, too. Their relationship had started out passionate enough, but over time she discovered she needed a lot more physical touch, deep bonding and adventure during sexual intimacy than he did. Jim was more conservative in this regard. Of course, the more Judith pushed him to be engaged, sexually and intellectually, the more he dug in his heels.

147

By the time we began having sessions, Jim was "narrow-minded and conservative—a real stick in the mud." Judith was heartbroken.

She fantasized about being with someone outside her marriage for the passionate sexual connection she desired in life, and felt shame about this—expressing concern about not wanting to "create more painful karma" in her relationships, and wanting to stay in integrity. Yet she was a passionate woman with desires and needs—Judith's speaking voice was smoky and seductive, which spoke volumes. She struck me as the kind of woman who could have sexual chemistry with just about anything and anyone at this point! For this vibrant and alive woman, this inner conflict was truly causing her intense amounts of distress and suffering.

Astrologically, Jim fit her fourth house Saturn signature in light and shadow. He was steady, reliable, loyal—and prone to rigidity and fear of change. He was a fourth house match, something that could indicate true love compatibility. But what was he matching, exactly? As we continued talking, eerie parallels emerged between how she experienced Jim and how she felt growing up in her family of origin.

Judith described growing up with conventional, religious parents who were very attached to the status quo. A passionate free-spirit, and a bit of a rule-breaker, she was often shamed and reprimanded for being colorful, outspoken about her passions and for stepping outside the lines. As a Caucasian woman, she had also committed the ultimate taboo act in her family system by falling in love with and marrying an African American man while in her twenties. This had happened decades ago, but the aftershock had lingered in her family. Now, in her marriage today, Jim appeared to take on the role of disapproving parent(s) and Judith, the rebellious child.

She continually challenged Jim—with her study of astrology, new age interests, her "weirdness." Was she looking for the acceptance and belonging she never received from her parents, from Jim? As we worked together, over time we stumbled upon the idea of doing ancestral work (see *Dancing with Skeletons* next) and she made an even deeper link between her oppressive experience of marriage, an old ancestral story and her upbringing. As she addressed the damaging fear, ancestral guilt, shame and repression that ran deep in her family, this radically rocked her perception of her marriage dynamics.

While she and Jim ultimately divorced, Judith had made this unconscious family complex, conscious—which meant she was not doomed to repeat that pattern again. She could see how the pattern had unconsciously ruled her. Because of this, she now had a choice. The last time we spoke, she said she was the happiest she'd been, and, sometimes a gift of doing inner work, she was appreciating her parents for the very first time in her life.

Judith's story isn't unusual; for couples, it's common to hear "the very things I fell in love with about him/her is driving me nuts!" Carl Jung's concept of the disowned self is worth understanding: the self that is deemed so unacceptable is pushed into the unconscious. For instance, if our family thought we were too passionate and bold and so shamed us for it, later in life we might fall in love with a person who resembles that disowned self we could not express. Or we may turn our partner into our parent and act out the early family drama of rejection and abandonment all over again in order to heal it. The psyche seeks wholeness. We experience relationship conflict to take back our projections and heal. Only then can we experience the freedom and fulfillment our heart most wants.

Judith didn't want to experience another failed marriage. She was a woman with a deep sense of integrity and loyalty, so also felt tremendous guilt around the decision to part ways with Jim. The fourth house is so deeply wedded to the idea of making a lifelong commitment to one person, till death do us part, and Saturn takes its vows very seriously.

Yet sometimes, for evolutionary reasons, we need to separate from the very mates who once felt "like home" to us, or still do. When dynamics just aren't supporting growth for one or both people any longer, it doesn't make sense to continue. Uprooting such a bond is deeply uncomfortable. The fourth house holds the part of us that urges us toward creating "forever bonds," and yet sometimes that runs counter to our Soul's need to evolve.

Dancing with Skeletons

"If you cannot get rid of the family skeleton, you may as well make it dance." - George Bernard Shaw

If you have run up against a mysterious blockage you cannot explain, consider asking your ancestors for help. The first rule of receiving any help from the Spirit world is simple: *Ask*. You have to ask. Then, receive. Allow your imagination and intuition to lead the way.

Because of the connections we had already made between the way she was raised in a rigid, shaming family and the nature of the man she had married, I had wondered if ancestral energies were at play in Judith's life. I told her about a little experiment I had done. I had been experiencing a season of frustration, futility and despair, and I wasn't sure why. One day, while sitting in our hot tub, the thought occurred to me, "These problems may not be your own." Minutes later, I received an email from a girlfriend about Constellation Therapy, which featured that exact phrase! (Constellation Therapy is a therapy that intuitively channels energies of ancestral and family dynamics to illuminate current mysterious conflicts).

This prompted a line of inquiry for me. I decided I would experimentally call in my ancestors and ask for their help. I lit some candles, centered for a few minutes and then spoke aloud: "I'm in quite a bit of pain and need your help. Ancestors, living or alive, if there is something you took to the grave that you need freeing through me, something you want to be heard, I am listening and I will do my best to help." I silently asked to know their regrets and frustrations. I told them I was willing to listen and do what I humanly could. Then I waited, with pen and paper, ready for action.

I wrote down the words as they came. First came my maternal grandmother, who shared the words and feelings "trapped," "powerless," "I don't know what to do," "desperate"—words I had been using without a clear source for the feelings. Writing these words helped my intense feelings soften. Another ancestor came through, my paternal grandfather, a concert pianist and band leader, who reminded me of my creative gifts, as well as my maternal great-great-grandmother, a real estate agent by day and poet by night. I had been feeling creatively blocked and this acknowledgment of artistic gifts in my lineage validated this part of me that lives to create.

As the words fell on the page, I somehow knew their author(s). I could feel the energy and their story unfold through the feeling contained in each word, without ever needing to know the details.

The next day I began to feel a shift, a lightness. Miraculously, simply acknowledging their frustrations and gifts cleared it entirely. Honest acknowledgement always clears stuck or blocked energy. When, with humility and openness, we connect with our Soul and ask to be guided to the Truth, we will be led there. Similar to Devi, I somehow knew the blockage I was experiencing wasn't just mine. I trusted that knowing enough to voice it to Spirit, and ask for guidance.

Judith listened to my retelling of this experiment, and it prompted her own. She invoked the presence of ancestral energies by creating an art object made of items from her female lineage. This act also initiated an automatic writing call and response process whereby she was able to identify an ancestor, born in 1563, whom she named "Sarah." Sarah was a Crusader who was ostracized by her family for her fiery sexuality when she fell in passionate love with a man who wasn't available to her—which was also a theme for Judith.

Below, Judith recounts her experience. It's a beautiful example of the powerful healing possible when we ask for help from our ancestors and how using ancestral objects, art-making and ritual facilitates this.

"I created a small art piece, a feminine assemblage of crimson raffia hair, a gown made from a beautiful paisley scarf I had been given by my maternal grandmother as a Christmas gift—which Grandmother had graciously returned to my mother so she could die unencumbered with material things and so I could wear the scarf that had never been removed from the gift box. The feet of the art piece were beautifully adorned in a hand-crafted pair of Cydwoq heels. These scraps, pieced together, I fondly began to call the 'wall woman.'.

"Once visibly present, I initiated a line of healing inquiry into my maternal lineage. I made an instant connection between Sarah's shame and loss and my own. As an adult woman, I had been rejected by my family for following the passions of my twenty-four-year-old heart when I married a black man I met while serving as a soldier in the U.S. Army in Mannheim, Germany. I bore a son conceived out of wedlock with a man not accepted by my white German Lutheran family, causing more familial guilt.

"It became curious to me how all three women (mother, grandmother, Sarah) suffered sexual shame within their families. An excruciating psychological pain plagued each one of them and has been ongoing for nearly five hundred years! My mother was scorned by the very grandmother who once owned but never wore the paisley scarf, scorned for carrying me out of wedlock. My mother had been deeply shamed by her own mother for becoming pregnant before marriage.

"My entire life I have carried a huge sense of guilt and shame. When I became old enough to understand my mother's psychological plight, my aunts confided (my mother's story) in me. I grew up often feeling unwanted by my parents, and a source of their desperation, but insights from my aunties helped me release self-blame for their anger, frustration.

"My conception, during which my mother experienced shame and hid her own passionate sexual nature, had been the family sore spot since the beginning—or perhaps a story repeated with origins from Sarah in the sixteenth century. The circle of shame and sexual frustration was handed down from the Reformation era through

Sarah to my mother in the late 1950s and then finally it fell to me. I am the one who finally asked for healing beyond time."

Exercise: Call in Your Ancestors

Art-making is a fantastic way to call in an ancestor and/or their story. It's great if you have some items that belonged to them, since physical items do resonate with their energy, but it's not necessary. If they are ready to talk through you, they will. Here are some more thoughts about connecting:

-Automatic writing. You can ask, as I did, "I am listening. What would you like me to know? What can I help you (and me!) to energetically clear?" Trust what comes through you, be it words, feelings or impulses. Truly, ask and you shall receive. The rule of thumb with Spirit is simply to ask.

-You may connect with someone you did not actually know. Ask them to identify their self. What year are they alive? What is happening in their world at this time? Are they married? Do they have children? Are they appearing to you because they share similarities with you?

-Know they may give you a name, and details, which may or may not be verifiable. This can certainly challenge the analytical left-brained among us! Set the intention to suspend mental analysis and simply trust what presents. Play. Act as if you are being told a story, perhaps one you never knew.

-Be creative. You can ask to see the world through your ancestors' eyes. One technique I learned for past life regression, which can certainly work for this: Relax. Close your eyes. In your mind's eye, see your feet. What shoes are you wearing? Are you wearing any? What clothes? Then, what does the ground you are standing on look like? When you look up, what do you see?

-Notice the feelings that arise for you. Write those down. Sometimes it's the feelings we feel that tell the entire story. For instance, icy cold rage. When I felt that, I instantly flashed on a great-grandmother. Now I associate that feeling with particular issues she faced, and knowing only a little of her story, I was able to piece together an intuitive picture.

Mars, Jupiter and Uranus Therapy

Although extremely uncomfortable, it's possible to be born into a family with whom we have nothing in common. In this case, our greatest virtues of character make themselves known by being paired with family members who demonstrate the exact opposite! When it comes to the family we incarnate with, there are truly no accidents.

If the fourth house describes our most influential parent, Donna's Mars, Jupiter and Uranus conjunction painted the picture of a parent with a forceful, unpredictable nature. Donna grew up with a father who was domineering, temperamental and quite wealthy, who bought others' affection through money and expressed favoritism.

By contrast, Donna was compassionate, sensitive, artistic and spiritual. And yet, here she was in this family whose values were one hundred and eighty degrees opposite. She saw how her father's money would turn other family members into compliant puppets who agreed to his demands, no matter how unreasonable. Despite being an artist who could really use it, she had always refused his offers of help. This put a large rift between her and her father (who couldn't control her with money), and her siblings.

When we first spoke, her father had just died, exacerbating this massive rift. Donna's father had left a significant amount of wealth to her siblings, to those who had complied with his wishes…and left nothing for her. To Donna, who had spent her whole life pulled between the forces of family belonging and following her own truth,

154

this felt like a final slap in the face. Not only had she lost her father in his death, she felt even more than ever before alienated by her siblings, who she wanted to turn to for support during this time of grief. They wouldn't acknowledge how demoralizing and awful this final act of leaving Donna out of his will was for her. She was shown no sympathy; she had refused to play along with the family rules.

Donna has Mars and Uranus in Cancer and Jupiter in Leo in the fourth house, which matched her experience of her father in the most negative extreme. Dad was archetypal in his embodiment of the raging warrior (Mars), overbearing tyrant (Uranus), and wealthy King (Jupiter in Leo). He had a powerful presence. He could give generously, and in an instant take his affections and money away.

Because she vehemently disagreed with the way family moved to the tune of her father's money and mood, she was labeled as angry (Mars), a rulebreaker (Uranus). In her flock, she was the black sheep non-conformist. She wouldn't play by the rules; she had boundaries and integrity! Individualistic and iconoclastic fourth house Uranians are born during a time when the family needs an electric jolt, a circuit breaker reset to shock the system into righting itself. Authenticity demands far more freedom than the family currently allows.

It's not easy to carry such strong archetypes, especially when it comes at the cost of shared feelings of family warmth and love. Donna also has a Cancer Sun in the third house, so the desire for close family and sibling bonds (third house) are deeply embedded in her value system. It hurt deeply to be cut out of her father's will, to experience insensitivity from her siblings, and yet these same people were allowing her to flex the muscle of her own authenticity and personal integrity. They presented her with the kind of hard choices that comprise the hero's journey. Would she choose to accept blood money, as her siblings did, or instead have the peace of sleeping at night with a clear conscience? In her Cancerian desire for sweet clan bonds, would she abandon her self? By choosing to stand against, instead of with, she did what many of us find extremely difficult to do: follow her Soul's truth, even at the risk of losing their affection.

Knowing a strong fourth house could mean the family complex was far bigger, extending back to other ancestors who faced similar conflicts, I asked: "Were there any rebels or outspoken outcasts in your lineage, ancestors you may or may not have known, who you could spiritually call on?" Immediately, Donna recalled a great-grandmother, a suffragette, who experienced extreme ostracism from the family for walking her own path, and whose independent spirit and progressive nature inspired Donna. In fact, Donna excitedly described a series of artworks she was actively working on involving this same grandmother. She left our session feeling empowered. She later wrote to say she received a healing dream that night.

Risking rejection, to stand in feminine truth and integrity, appeared to extend back and now forward in time to Donna!

Fourth house planets may bequeath to us something to resolve or redeem that is not just ours, but work we are doing on behalf of our entire lineage. At times this may not feel fair, but it can also feel extremely empowering and exciting. It is inspiring to feel that one's life is an answer to something far bigger. You may carry an answer your entire lineage has waited for! They may be cheering your inner work on from the other side this very minute.

And if you feel you've carried the family shadow for far too long, you certainly carry the family hero as well. After all, what is a hero if not someone who has the courage to bring the family shadow to light?

Exercise: Your Power Ancestor

Donna discovered a spiritual ally in her great-grandmother. After having such a difficult time with family, this put wind underneath her wings. What a resource! It was like finding out she had Wonder Woman in her lineage.

What if someone in your lineage has stood exactly where you are standing, too, and is ready to offer you their wisdom from the other side? Consider you have someone equally powerful and important in your lineage. There is someone who has faced the troubling issues you face in your life. They may have something to share with you, a gift to bequeath to you, a path forward, a light, a way through. With some creativity, intuition and investigation, you can find that person and unlock the treasures that lay waiting for you.

You might intuitively know who they are already, right now, or you may need to take a little journey to find them. Here's a method for doing that:

-Get in a quiet space. Light some candles or dim the lights. Lay down or comfortably sit. Set the intention to meet your power ancestor.

-Feel your body. Feel the contact of your skin on the chair or bed. Breathe. Slow down. Do whatever practices you need that center and ground you.

-Take a journey down a lazy river or stream. You are on a comfortable marshmallow raft. Imagine the coolness of the water as you trail it with your hand, birds singing, the slow movement of trees as you pass them by.

-Your raft arrives at a little island. You slowly disembark and notice someone sitting on a bench underneath an apple tree, waiting just for you.

-What do you feel in their presence? Your feelings will tell most of the story.

-You can ask them questions like, "What would you like to tell me?" They are your power ancestor, are here to share something important with you.

-What do you feel you two might have in common? What wisdom can they share with you about this issue you have and that they know so well?

-Stay light. Don't be in your mind or head. Be receptive to what arises.

-When you are done, thank them for sharing their wisdom, for their insight.

-Wave goodbye. Tell them you will visit again (if you will!). Embark on your raft. Slowly float downstream back to your waking consciousness.

-When you return to waking, record your impressions in a journal.

Chiron Therapy

Cece was a powerful healer. She received psychic impressions quite often, especially through her rich dream life (Pisces in the fourth house), where she connected with instructive teachers and healers who gave her information she could use in her waking life in synchronous and magical ways. She periodically sent me pictures of stones, crystals, which her dream teachers would instruct her to place around her house! This rich world of meaningful symbolism, spiritual touchstones and magic literally kept her warm at night. Lately, especially, when human relationship disappointed.

Cece's asteroid Chiron (in Pisces) was in her fourth house. Although Chiron is an asteroid and not a planet, if it is strongly placed in any sector of the natal chart I will often retell aspects of the myth. Myth can be very evocative, drawing forth new awareness.

Until he was inadvertently caught in the crossfire of someone else's battle and injured by a poison arrow at his heel, Chiron was an immortal Centaur leader who enjoyed his freedom. Yet this unfair and deeply painful wound inflicted by life itself changed his life course entirely. Chiron spent the rest of his life searching far and wide for healing. In his healing journey he acquired many healing tools, becoming an expert in many different holistic techniques (Chiron is in the word *chiro*-practic). Like many who suffer a meaningless act of injustice and/or insult to the physical body and are forced into a lifelong search of looking for cures and answers that don't readily arrive, Chiron was challenged to continually search for healing without necessarily finding an ultimate cure, and to live life undefined by limitation, not as a victim. His experience with suffering, pain, sickness and injustice gave him great humanity and compassion for the suffering we all experience while in earthly bodies. Chiron offered what he'd learned to others, gaining respect and renown as a wise healer. Ultimately, the ageless immortal being, who knew his search could go on forever, asked to be made mortal so he could die. Chiron willingly gave up his immortality, trading places with Prometheus, and died. Zeus/Jupiter granted his wish.

As you might suspect from the myth, Chiron is prominent in the charts of people who undergo dramatic health and life reversals and spiritual crises. The asteroid is also extremely prominent in the charts of healers and teachers (if you, too, identify with this story, you are definitely Chironian). Cece was Chironian. Like many with a strong Chiron, Cece had extended moments of wanting to leave this earthly plane. Chiron in the fourth house suggests alienation and estrangement from family, and, indeed, Cece felt herself to be very different from her biological family. As true for many healers, Cece did not feel she was born into her Soul family. Her biological family was a continual source of pain and alienation.

As Saturn began to transit Chiron by square, Cece's beloved father died. Her father was the one bright spot in Cece's challenging family experience, so his death was a huge blow for her. Her grief left her feeling tender, exposed, orphaned. It's a common experience to feel orphaned when we lose a parent. Throughout her grieving process, Cece began realizing her family role more clearly. She had been the only truth-teller in a family system maintained by falsity, lies, dramas and secrecy. This realization left her feeling more alone than ever during her time of need, but it was also a gift of clear-seeing.

During this time, she also began dating a man who was adopted, a true orphan. This man, however fun and exciting to be around for her, also ran hot and cold, one day showing up, and then totally gonzo the next. He continually triggered her abandonment wounds. She had a choice: she could turn him into the person who might reject her as her family did and go crazy trying to win his affection, or she could see him as a reflection of what it was time to heal.

I suggested it was time to befriend her inner orphan. She was knee deep in the underworld of learning to love herself unconditionally. This meant no longer viewing love as conditional and reliant on external sources. Once, her family's love, attention and affection were necessary for her survival, but no longer. Cece was no longer a child. Saturn transits remind us that we've grown, matured and changed. It was time to withdraw her love projections from family members. She was no longer dependent on them for anything, including love. It was time to understand that Love itself is Self as Source.

As she owned her own Divine sovereignty, there would be potential for creating a new family, one more accurately reflecting herself as healer and teacher. Her true Soul's mates would be healers, teachers, mentors, those who are different, living on the fringe of convention. A Chiron tribe may resemble a montage of colourful characters, a shaman, a homeless woman, a light-worker, an empath, an artist. In other words, a Chironic tribe consists of compassionate, creative, interesting people who are very intimate with the human condition. They've lived some colourful, and often painful, experiences and have integrated that into a healing offering or service. Such members not only bring medicine to those with Chiron in the fourth, but create a more spiritually appropriate definition of family for them.

I did not hear back from Cece. I could tell she felt she was at the end of her rope. Sometimes Saturn (and fourth house) transits are like that. For myself, I felt I held the energy of transiting Saturn for her, which isn't always comfortable. Saturn can bring us the bracing clarity we need, but it can feel like an icy cold bucket of water. Yet if we think we're drowning, Saturn can help us realize that we aren't drowning and that we are the rescuer we seek.

Where Chiron falls in the chart, it is easy to find oneself in the enchanted forest standing before a door we very much want to walk through and feel locked out. We may feel cursed. We find it easy to feel like a victim. Yet, just like mythic Chiron, we are the only one who can turn our suffering into a wisdom path. With Chiron, the disease also contains the cure. The two cannot be separated, so we must learn to use it. Suffering is inevitable. With chironic pain, we learn to use our suffering as a path of transformation.

Your Soul's Mates: Calling in Your Chosen Tribe

Clearly, in life, not everyone gets an ideal family experience. *We're not supposed to.* Your fourth house shows what your Soul, for evolutionary growth purposes, wants to experience from family and its members, both in shadow and in light. Yes, this often runs counter to the Ego's desires. When we appear to be learning through opposites—through what we don't have in family, where we were neglected, abused, mistreated—this can feel painful and unfair. We can choose to heal, though, and take a broader perspective.

Family is not responsible for our spiritual growth. We are. Once we come to terms with the truth of what is, we are ready to step out of victimhood and create. Like the Goldilocks and the three bears story, your fourth house clearly spells out what is better, best and ultimately just right for you, but you get the free will to decide, to choose, which version. For instance, with Chiron in the fourth, a family of healers and folks with perspective, who understand the suffering inherent to life and are actively part of the solution, is a better choice than being stuck in that painful Achilles heel of wanting things to be different (with family) than what it is. Every planet offers options. It's empowering to choose "just right" for you.

161

Here are some questions for reflection. Now that you've learned more about your fourth house, you are more than equipped to honestly answer them. Work through these questions to free yourself up to attract a just right tribe!

Is my biological family my spiritual family/tribe?

Now that I can better understand my fourth house, what are the qualities of those I consider my spiritual or Soul family/tribe? What does my fourth house archetype(s) suggest might be the best fit for me?

Do I have any survival strategies and conditioning from childhood that could be impeding my ability to attract my Soul's mates?

Have I been giving my dysfunctional, biological (not spiritual) family members the same privileges and loyalty as I would a family in which I feel reciprocity, love and respect? If so, how can I take better care of and honor myself (boundaries: saying no, limiting contact, separating from them etc.)?

Do I regularly cave in to pressure to do things for my family that act against my values or in any way feels out of alignment in my Soul? Can I see that I pay a price for that? What price do I pay?

Do I still expect or want my family to see, understand, listen to, celebrate and honor me in ways they've never been able to historically? Can I see how this expectation or desire has hurt me in the past and continues to?

Am I still trying to get this family member to love and understand me? Am I holding onto a fantasy of our relationship that never existed?

What resources was I forced to develop as a result of my difficult family experience? Can I turn the coin to the other side and see that my fourth house has given me strengths? Can I see how, without these "negative" experiences, I might not have appreciated or recognized these valuable inner strengths and gifts?

Can I view a troubled family relationship from a higher perspective? Can I imagine this person as an actor, playing a starring role in my spiritual development, helping me to better develop weak or vulnerable areas?

Can I see that every time I was neglected, humiliated, shamed or treated un-lovingly that it was their projection, a reflection of that family members' relationship to their self? (For instance, if they doubted and feared my love, they were afraid of abandonment). Can I commit to not only intellectually understanding this, but also knowing and living this as a truth? Can I embody this truth so I no longer perceive myself as the object of their pain - or anyone's, for that matter? Can I deeply know that they have only ever been the subject of their own ridicule, shame, rejection and pain (not me)?

Is there one good reason (the only good reason being peace) to keep an antagonistic relationship going with a family member? Am I willing to take responsibility for letting go of my attachment to trying to get something from them that they were never able to give?

Can I give myself permission to only be motivated by self-love (not guilt), ease (not stress) and grace (not pressure) in all matters pertaining to family? If I don't feel this, can I give myself permission to opt out?

Conclusion: The House of Belonging

"This is the temple of my adult aloneness, and I belong to that aloneness as I belong to my life…" - David Whyte, *The House of Belonging*

I was showing my Jupiter tropical hideaway home to a new friend. As we strolled the property together, she exclaimed, "Wow, you have found your zen zone! If I lived here, I would never leave the house." I chuckled, since this was intentional. I love being at home. I work here, I live here. I love my solitude. I can honestly say that while I used to feel alone, I don't anymore. Like many introverts, I tend to feel more connected to myself when I am alone, and more distracted by external energies, from myself, when I'm not.

"I couldn't live here, though…" she went on. "As much as I wish I could, I'm trying not to be so much of a hermit. My friends are on my case to get out in the world more." I said, "Well, I've stopped going against my natural inclinations. I embrace my inner hermit!"

Much changed when I moved to Hawaii. As I gave myself such big permission to follow the path that felt most authentic for me, many of the old concepts I'd had about who I *should* be just fell away. One of the more remarkable things that changed was the sense of belonging that had eluded me my whole life. I had long associated belonging with belonging to a person, friendships, group, place or mission. I was looking to external forms for what could only independently arise from within. I hadn't yet figured out (I had intellectually understood, but not actually energetically embodied) that belonging was not tied to anyone or anything outside of me.

Perhaps the feeling of having been dropped by the stork on the wrong doorstep had made belonging all the more important to dial in. Yet as I have grown more honest with myself, as my identity has expanded and I've become more awake and aware, I can see that I was looking for something that nothing external could ever give. Belonging is not something you can get from another person, place, a perfect childhood, home or partnership. Belonging is something you can only give yourself. When you take the time to get to know who you truly are, you eventually understand that the only real belonging any of us ever needs to do is belong to our Self, our Divinity.

After all, at the end of life, we don't take our home, tribe, or our body with us. We take our Soul, our innermost Self—all we ever need. We are more like turtles in this way. We carry home within.

Paradoxically, I can see how this deepest recentering with belonging only to my deeper self could occur only when I became honest about needing to align with all of these elements that were foundationally askew: I needed to get fed up with tolerating what had become intolerable, and allow myself to want more from my life. I had to put an end old childhood survival patterns, like putting other people's wants and desires before my own. The stakes were high. In deciding to put myself first, I risked losing the person I most loved.

To free oneself is a revolution, in the planetary sense of the word. Seeing how far we've deviated from who we truly are is the first step of living a more authentic, Soul-centered, life. To get back to who we truly are, we usually have to clear up habits of misunderstanding-perceptions, beliefs, old conditioning - keeping us imprisoned. Then, we have the freedom to choose from a truer place. Like a baby learning to walk all over again, we may get up and fall down a bit at first, but eventually the truer choice becomes the most natural one.

This is coming home. No picket fence can give this to us. No perfect partner can provide us with the safety, completion or bliss we seek.

Which brings me back to my quiet kid. She's a sensitive, imaginative, gifted, extremely empathic and intuitive introvert. But you knew that, right? I am happy to report she now one hundred percent loves all of this about herself. No trying to be something she is not. If she wants to stay home, we do. I am happy as a clam doing my fourth house things: writing, reading, and other various hobbies I enjoy in the privacy of my own self. I don't need numbers of people to validate my existence (please, no!). I am happy with my dog, and my partner, who travels a lot. I don't judge myself for not being more involved in community affairs, or more active in politics, or for not having a wider friend network, even when others judge themselves. Not to say things can change. If I ever feel the desire to do any of that, I will.

When I look in the mirror of the world, I notice others showing up to remind me of my newfound liberation. Clients who think there's something wrong with them when they only have one or two close friends, or they aren't active members of their community, or feel guilty they're not working on solving the world's ills. I look at those same clients' charts, see a strongly placed Moon, and ask, "Why are you telling yourself that you should be an activist or more social, when you're a healer and a poet at heart? Why not use your gift for poetry to activate hearts?" Meanwhile, my dog walking pal neighbor tells me he is sick and crazy from watching the news but he must keep watching because "I don't want to bury my head in the sand."

I instantly think, oh, but getting buried in sand can be fun! There are so many beaches in Oahu, fantastic for doing just that! I gaze at the shoreline, wondering how long it has been since he's visited one.

There goes my fourth house again. I will advocate for doing what feels right, true, natural, joyful. From this space, there are no more "shoulds" or external pressures, no old conditioning, obligation, guilt, doubt or self-judgment. Just self-acceptance and presence. Just following what feels right and true for me. I do what feels natural, right, right now. Which is always what I truly want to do, anyhow.

I belong to me.

It's a remarkable, freeing thing to own. I am so grateful for the booty of Jupiter: my loving Soul mate of a husband, the beautiful tropical hideaway and this amazing life I now have in Hawaii, but none of it belongs to me, nor do I belong to it. I belong to myself.

I am at home in myself.

And this is the most liberating feeling in the world.

Come Home to Yourself:
An Intuitive Energy Practice

Here's an energy practice to help you come back home to yourself.

"Come home," calls a distant voice from deep inside you.

Perhaps you've been feeling more emotional lately, or your attention has been too focused outside yourself. Don't worry, this will be easy. Just set the intention to withdraw from the external world. Let go of concern about what's going on outside of you, about anything but you, right now.

This time is for you and only for you.

Go inside your body, notice tension, and relaxation. Feel the tight walls of muscle around your stomach. The energy gathered inside your pelvis. The relaxed muscles of your legs and feet. Feel your feet on the ground. Your breath, how you're holding it slightly high, or breathing in your belly.

Notice your energy. Is it running fast, or comfortably slow? Don't judge it. If you'd like to slow down, simply ask your energy body: What would it be like to slow down? What would it feel like to relax? Then pause, and wait a minute or less for the answer, which will be a subtle feeling of relaxation.

Take a few deep breaths, come back into yourself. Settle into your pelvic bowl. Release what's not yours. Feel the fullness of your own energy here.

Ground your energy. Imagine your trunk is the trunk of an ancient tree, rooted into the earth. You are eternally: solid, safe, stable, grounded. The wind may rustle your leaves, rain may wet your branches, but nothing changes this fact. Take a few moments to deeply connect with this truth.

Now, feel your feet become roots, and send those roots deep into the rich, moist Earth. Let them expand as far, wide and deep as you like.

Do not be afraid to take up space, to nourish yourself with big, round, juicy, long roots. Feel the moist dirt cradle your roots, protecting, connecting, nourishing you for as long as you call this planet your home.

"Come home," calls the voice again, now closer. This time you are far more present to the voice. It is your Soul's voice. You realize it hasn't grown closer, it was always here. You've simply taken the time to draw closer to it.

What an amazing discovery to realize that you are always right here for you, that all you have to do to feel this way is slow down and connect within.
Your imagination opens, opening you to everything you love…

"Come home…" What do you love? Maybe it's the smell of fresh baked cookies, the silvery glow of the full moon over a field of fragrant lavender, dozing in a fluffy feather bed under a midnight blue starry sky, or curling up into the warm, furry body of your favorite animal or snuggle buddy.

"Come home…" You imagine a field of rich golden light, the warmth of a distant star, the softest cotton brushing against your skin, reclining under a huge oak tree next to a shimmering and still emerald-turquoise lake.

You start to feel so light. You are expanding into your innate Divinity, you are filled with light. So much light. So much warmth, connection, safety.

"Come home…" You now decide to release anything that is no longer aligned with this Divine Soul that you are. You do not need worry, regret, sadness, fear. There is no place for it here. They are nothing more than passing clouds, phenomenon that never change anything about you or your path.

"Come home..." You imagine a beautiful Mother Goddess appearing to you, offering you the ease of total acceptance and full permission. Permanent permission to be exactly as you are, always. There is nothing to do, nowhere to go, nowhere to be. You are perfect. You are unconditionally loved.

A profound peace settles over your body. You are safe. You are loved. All is well. This is always and forever true. You know this. Connect with this truth for as long as you like. Steep in the peace, bliss and ease of your true nature.

Welcome home.

Appendix: How to Locate the Fourth House in Your Birth Chart

1. Head over to www.astro.com and enter your birth details (birth date, time, and place) to receive a free copy of your birth chart.

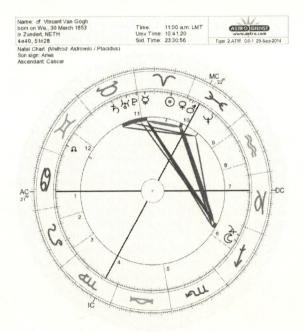

Name: ♂ Vincent Van Gogh
born on We., 30 March 1853
in Zundert, NETH
4e40, 51n28
Natal Chart (Method: Astrowiki / Placidus)
Sun sign: Aries
Ascendant: Cancer

Time: 11:00 a.m. LMT
Univ Time: 10:41:20
Sid. Time: 23:30:56

ASTRO DIENST
www.astro.com
Type: 2.ATW 0.0-1 29-Sep-2014

2. Your chart will look something like this (this is Vincent van Gogh's chart). What is this beautiful madness? Imagine taking your

first breath and looking upward. This is a snapshot of the heavens from the exact place, at the precise moment, you were born.

3. There are 12 constellations organizing our sky, reflected in the 360-degree circle of your birth chart, divided into twelve sectors, or astrological houses. Each house corresponds to a different area of life

You may notice that house sizes vary. Some are big while others are small, due to the location in which you were born (the further north or south you were born from the equator, the more extreme the differences in house sizes will be). Each zodiac sign is always allotted 30 degrees (30x12=360 degrees of a circle), but some houses will contain more or less than that, with the degrees of one zodiac sign spilling into the next house or beginning midway at a house cusp. Beginners, take note: the size of your house of "love" or "money" is not a reflection of how much or how little you will have of either!

4. Using the following diagram, imagine the path of the Sun over the course of a day as it travels through the sky map, or your birth chart. The Sun rises at dawn at the easternmost point, or the cusp of the first house, called the Ascendant (Rising, or ASC, as seen here).

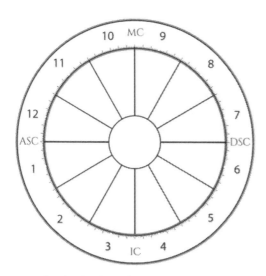

The Sun then travels clockwise, through the twelfth and then eleventh houses until it reaches the cusp of the tenth house or the

Midheaven (MC) at high noon. It keeps moving, as Sun gradually descends through the ninth, eighth and seventh houses, from afternoon and evening, to the westernmost point of the chart, the cusp of the seventh house, or Descendant (DSC), where it sets. Commencing its progress into the sixth, fifth, and then fourth house, it is now very dark. By midnight, Sun is at the southernmost point of the chart, the fourth house cusp or the Imum Coeli (IC).

Now, look at your own chart. Can you find your fourth house?

5. What is the sign on the cusp of your fourth house? Look to the sign beginning, or on the cusp, of your fourth house. If you don't know them, you can find the symbols for each zodiac sign, Aries through Pisces, located in the right column. Your cusp sign shows your motivation and approach toward this area of life.

Sun	☉	♈	Aries
Moon	☽	♉	Taurus
Mercury	☿	♊	Gemini
Venus	♀	♋	Cancer
Mars	♂	♌	Leo
Jupiter	♃	♍	Virgo
Saturn	♄	♎	Libra
Uranus	♅	♏	Scorpio
Neptune	♆	♐	Sagittarius
Pluto	♇	♑	Capricorn
North Node	☊	♒	Aquarius
South Node	☋	♓	Pisces

6. Are there any planets in your fourth house? To find the planet(s) in your fourth house, refer to the left hand of the column.

Planets indicate energy and action, so the more planets you have in any given house, the more energy you expend in that area of life. What if you have no planets in the fourth house? That's okay. There are 10 planets (including the Moon) and twelve houses, so no one will have a planet in every house. Houses that don't have planets may be empty, but they are not lifeless. The goings-on of this house are mediated by the sign on the cusp of the house, that zodiac sign's ruling planet, and the planets moving through that house (transits).

7. Do you want to know more? My favorite beginner books are *Astrology for Yourself* by Demetra George and Douglas Bloch, and *The Inner Sky* by Steven Forrest.

About the Author

Jessica Shepherd is the author of *A Love Alchemist's Notebook: Magical Secrets for Drawing Your True Love into Your Life* (Llewellyn 2010), *Karmic Dates & Momentary Mates: The Astrology of the Fifth House* (Moonkissd 2014), and *Venus Signs: Discover Your Erotic Strengths and Secret Desires Through Astrology* (Llewellyn 2015). Jessica lives in Honolulu, HI with her husband, John, dog, Magnus, and cat, Obi. She offers intuitive sessions to help you connect with your True Self. To learn more visit www.moonkissd.com.

Made in the USA
Middletown, DE
04 August 2024

58477958R00111